Life in the
Out Lane

Life in the *Out* Lane

The Bumpy Road
Toward Love, Laughter
and Enlightenment

Sharon Kant-Rauch

ISBN 13: 978-0692969700

Articles originally printed in the *Tallahassee Democrat,* reprinted with permission.

"Sabbath Outing" from *Between the Two Rivers: Stories From the Red Hills to the Gulf,* edited by Susan Cerulean, Janisse Ray and Laura Newton (Tallahassee: Heart of the Earth, 2004), reprinted with permission.

Afterword by Noah Kant-Rauch originally written as an essay in 2011, reprinted with permission.

Published by CreateSpace

Edited by Julie Klein (JKlein-Editor.com)

Cover design by Mi Ae Lipe (whatnowdesign.com)

Cover art by Jim Warren (jimwarren.com)

Interior design by Julie Klein

Photograph by Steve Cannon

Printed in the United States of America

For Sophia, the next generation

Contents

Foreword   xi

Preface   xiii

What happens when little boys play mermaid?   1

The crime stories you read are only a violent fraction   4

Cops don't look at weekends as you probably do   7

An invisible sign declares: Women, beware   10

A day with David was even better than 'Lion King'   13

A pair of dashing pirates ready to take on the world   16

A closer look showed this bear was very Special   19

Who cares about sports? Now I do   22

A football game turns into a war when…   24

Digest these tales from a trip to the Bog of the Bug-Eating Plants   27

See Noah trot! See Mom run!   31

Galloping days have just begun for this parent   34

Time chatting in park adds grace to life   37

The tyranny of birthday parties   39

Between tears and rocket lectures, a nice family dinner   42

Child-care workers deserve decent pay   45

Guilt gets modern mothers nowhere   47

Pass the popcorn when you have 'One Life to Live'   50

Call now: Breast cancer waits for no one   53

Love and kindness can outshine the worst of hate   56

Some of us fry latkes *and* hang Christmas stockings   59

Her word around the house is going to the dogs   62

A God-filled moment can illuminate our lives   65

Family life recedes when fever intrudes   68

An 11-year-old's courage is contagious   70

It's a family tradition with wheels   73

A spiritual life comes in many guises 76
Life changes when son is at camp 79
We avert our eyes from sweatshop misery 82
Electronic beasts can rule a home 85
Terrible events leave parents numb, kids confused 88
Driven to distraction by furry, furtive invaders in the
    wall 91
Pacifist ideals are tested by terrorism 95
Silence reveals gunk, pearls 98
Spend time with the children of gays 102
Yours might be golf; mine is religion 105
God's voice could calm Middle East 108
Mothers know their value, and that's good enough 110
Let a child follow your spiritual lead 112
Homosexuality is an easy scapegoat for churches 114
Whole community must honor marriage
    commitment 116
Be thankful for the righteous among us 119
Abortion is a thorny issue for us all 121
His focus on peace hasn't wavered 124
Older and wiser, I now know to savor life 127
Worlds unfold outside the front door 129
Heart of a nomad beats within this mom 131
Fashion keeps a shackle on women 133
Remember, you look marvelous! 135
I am, like many Americans, filthy stinking rich 137
Watching with trepidation as friends lose their
    parents 139
Required giving misses important point 141
Sharing Mom's wheels could be cool 144
Tooth fairy may vanish, but she'll be back 147
Religion is a ripe subject for Hollywood 149
Sharing the load: From laundry to parenting duties 152
Suffering people need more than compassion 154

Anger and love surge in family storms   156
Adult friends give son a place in their world   159
Say a prayer as Israel buries its dead   161
Gays were silent on election's hot topic   163
Respect for Mom grows as years pass   165
Sabbath Outing   167
Punched by cancer, picked up by love   175
A bead up a 3-year-old's nose? 'Dora did it!'   177
Pardon me while I slow down for cancer   180
The sweet, the sad on Port St. Joe beach   182
What must we protect? Innocence, beauty   185
'Holy Night' sparkled beneath the stars   187
Bald head isn't a sign of bravery   189
Finding Isaac and a lot more   191
Picture this: A love story, 10 years later   193
When the gay issue hits home   195
Don't sit back and wait for change   198
In the park, with a child, God's blessing is revealed   200
Yearning leads us to God   202
A moment of peace emerges at a hospital   204
The kids (of lesbian moms) are all right   206
Village people salve more than cancer   208
Wonders come every day in ordinary ways   210
Dates and prayer go a long way in a marriage   212
Aunt Vicki brings the banquet   215
Do religious people make better neighbors?   218
Retreats allow us to move toward God   220
Camping with 9-year-old was magical trip   223
Pain, praise find expression in the psalms   226
'So Whats' should review research about benefits of
    religion   229
Are you picky or easily satisfied?   231
Stopping rape starts with respecting women   234
We're so much better if we aren't alone   237

Think what churches could do   240

Entertainment crosses the line to depravity   243

A few people help make a city great   246

Sometimes there's virtue in just listening   249

Human element outlasts memory   252

Me and my little Aliner   254

There's a special magic in breaking bread together   258

Start now to stop campus assaults   261

First camping trip brings laughter   265

Use High Holy Days to consider the Holy Land   269

Women must get past being objects   273

Mind your own busyness   277

Women can model religious chutzpah   280

A holiday tale of a girl, her dogs   283

Marriage is changing for everyone.   285

What children want most is to make their own way   288

Tragic events can lead to understanding and
compassion   291

Women need a cave of their own   293

Election stirs up the soul of protest   295

Accept the challenge of Hanukkah lights   297

Afterword   299

Foreword

Maybe someday I'll be asked to write the foreword for a book I can't stand, and I'll spend sleepless nights trying to concoct ways I can wiggle off the hook. Thank heavens, this is not that day, that book, that hook. This one's a gem.

If you love Sharon Kant-Rauch (and who doesn't?), you're going to love this book. If you don't know Sharon before you open it, afterward you'll feel as if you do.

These 110 stories are like Sharon: compact, powerful and lovingly honest.

They let you peer inside the life and the heart of a mom, wife, believer, citizen, good-natured agitator, nature lover, cancer survivor, lesbian, woman, friend.

They're brief but compelling glimpses that first appeared in the *Tallahassee Democrat*, where Sharon was a reporter and editor for 21 years. She thought newspapers should tell the stories of everyday life — which she did through her stories but also, effortlessly, through her columns.

In person, Sharon is infectiously upbeat and often leaves you smiling, just as many of these stories do. But she's not afraid to let down her guard, to portray herself in a less than flattering light, to wrestle with issues the rest of us sidestep, to show how her thinking has evolved.

Even though Sharon's not a fussy writer, you might wear out your felt-tip pen if you start underlining memorable passages. Here's one I particularly like: "She felt she moved in and out of safe environments as she would move in and out of air-conditioned buildings. Being gay was OK here, not OK there."

Maybe my favorite column in this book ends with three short sentences, all beginning with "I am." I don't want to write them out in full here, lest I steal any of their thunder. Let's just say you might want to make sure you're seated near a box of Kleenex.

And if you're not already, at that point you'll become a member of the Sharon Kant-Rauch fan club.

Ron Hartung

Preface

These columns, written over a 25-year period, are being published as a book for one main reason: my children. In 2005, I was diagnosed with stage 3 breast cancer. My kids were 15, 9 and 2 at the time. If I died, what would they remember about me?

I was haunted by this thought, even as I clocked in year after year of survival. Then, a few years ago, I looked through a cardboard box of my columns and realized the most important things I wanted them to know about me were already in writing. My columns covered a lot about families — our family in particular — but they also included my thoughts on religion, nature, community, feminism and gay rights.

I suddenly wanted to put them together in a book so I could give each child a copy. As I write this, my first grandchild, Sophia, is on the way. This book is dedicated to her.

But I'm also hoping the general public will enjoy reading these columns again. People still talk to me about my columns, even though it's been five years since I left the *Tallahassee Democrat*. If nothing else, I hope a few columns will make readers laugh.

At the end of the book, I've included an essay written by my son Noah when he was in high school. I found it during the time I was putting together this book. Reading what life was like for him during a critical time in our family moved me deeply. I think it will move you, too.

I titled the book "Life in the Out Lane: The Bumpy Road Toward Love, Laughter and Enlightenment" because I have seldom chosen the middle road. Instead, I've put myself out there — as a lesbian, a feminist, a radical person of faith. A bumpy ride, for sure, but a great way to travel.

I'd like to thank Ron Hartung, editor par excellence. Many writers will say how certain editors improved their work — which Ron certainly did for me during the almost 20 years we worked together at the *Tallahassee Democrat*. But he also did something else — he encouraged me. Writers are supersensitive types who can easily be deflated. While Ron would often challenge me, he always did so in a gentle, supportive way. I wouldn't have had the courage to be a columnist without him.

This book wouldn't have been put together without the help of Julie Klein and Mi Ae Lipe. Julie typed all the articles into a manuscript, did a final copyedit, and got it into printable form. Mi Ae designed the fabulous cover. I love the results!

I also want to thank my parents, Bob and Barbara Rauch, for the love they've shown me all of my life. Their dependability, caring and generosity have set a good example for me and my whole family. I feel so fortunate that they came to live in Tallahassee in 2005.

I am deeply grateful to my three children — David, Noah and Jenna. Each one brings me happiness, challenges me and motivates me to keep growing. I am honored to be one of their moms.

Most of all I want to thank my wife, Terry. Every day I marvel at the life we have created together. She is my biggest blessing.

What happens when little boys play mermaid?

My child's favorite fantasy is being a mermaid — swimming through water, preening in the sun.

At 4 years old, dressing up in tights, a tutu and a multicolored clown's wig is another costume favorite.

But David also likes collecting rocks and bugs, digging holes to China and finding out everything he can about outer space and trains.

As a longtime feminist, it delights me that my child enjoys playing on both sides of the traditional gender fence.

But unlike female children, who are being encouraged — or at least not discouraged — to pursue nontraditional activities as they grow older, my son's days of trying out the female world are numbered.

Consider the headline above an advice column in the *Tallahassee Democrat* a few weeks ago: "Should a parent worry if a son only wants to play with girls' toys?"

The problem, according to the worried parent, was that a 5-year-old boy played constantly with girls' toys, and especially favored a pink princess costume.

This child must be like David, I thought. Although cowboy boots and hat are mixed together in a box with his other dress-up clothes, he prefers to put on a discarded women's bathing suit and be a mermaid.

And as I read Beverly Mills' advice column, which went to great lengths to cover all bases — from girl toys "will make them better fathers" to speculating about sexual preference if the girl play was too extreme — I wondered, would we ever see a headline like that with parents worrying about their girls playing with boys' toys?

I doubt it.

For a girl to want to play sports, be a doctor, climb trees and learn science only elevates her status — she's more like a boy, which society still considers the norm.

But if a boy wants to play house, dress in a princess costume, pamper his dolls and bake cookies, he's straying from that norm and being "like a girl," and therefore deviant.

The real problem is that society values traditional female activities less than male ones.

If most people thought cooking dinner was as important as putting out a fire, we wouldn't have worried parents asking these kinds of toy-appropriate questions.

So, for as much time as I have spent in my adult life trying to cheer on females to be whatever they want to be, I now find I must rally to my son's side, too.

It's not something I thought I would have to do. Even without a father, I thought David — a white, middle-class male — would be able to be anything he wanted.

But what if he prefers mermaids to Ninja Turtles?

Grown-ups are uncomfortable. Other children tease. At 4 years old, David is already beginning to absorb the disapproval.

Although he plays dress-up with his friends every chance he can get, he does so only behind his closed bedroom door.

"Only girls play dress-up," he confided in me one day.

In a few years, I'm sure even this clandestine play will become obsolete.

When my niece was 6, she could wear red pants, no shirt and a green sash around her head as she charged around being Rambo — and no one batted an eye.

I doubt the same would be true if, in two years, David dances out in his tutu.

I want it to be different. I want him to be able to dip into any activity, regardless of gender stereotypes.

With help from people like Fred, a child-care worker at David's preschool, that just might happen.

The boys were talking one day about how only girls wore dresses. To prove them wrong, Fred wore a skirt to school the next day.

I loved it. We need more males, young and old, to revel in "women's stuff," instead of sneering in disgust.

Think about what you could do. I don't want my little mermaid to leave me too soon.

June 1, 1993

The crime stories you read are only a violent fraction

A 9-year-old girl, upset that her parents didn't get her the videos she wanted, tries to hang herself. She still lies in the hospital, unconscious.

In front of two friends near Lake Ella, a man in his 20s shoots himself in the right temple with a .44-caliber Magnum. He dies.

Another man comes to the emergency room with a bullet lodged in his stomach. He says he was shot as he came out of a convenience store.

A man bashes his wife over the head with a ceramic cat, then hits her repeatedly in the face with his fist.

All of this happened in Tallahassee during the past two weeks. None of it was reported in the paper, on TV or on the radio.

Suicides, unless they're done publicly or the person is well-known, usually aren't reported — in deference to the family.

The reason for not reporting the other violent crimes is less lofty: They're just too common.

"Crime is growing to such an extent that what may have been newsworthy 10 years ago isn't anymore," says Officer Glenn Sapp, public-information officer for the Tallahassee Police Department. "We just see so much of it."

Police don't have time to do a press release on every crime in the city, and newspapers don't have room to print them.

Granted, we're not as bad as places like Miami, where crime reporters have been known to write a "Murder Roundup," a single story that includes a brief mention of the day's murder victims.

"Often assistant city editors, short on space and patience, would insist that I select and report only the 'major murder' of the day," wrote the legendary Edna Buchanan, former crime reporter for the *Miami Herald*, in her book "The Corpse Had a Familiar Face."

"I knew what they meant, but fought the premise. How can you choose?

"Every murder is major to the victim."

We're not that bad yet in Tallahassee. Murders still get good coverage, but other crimes and violence must be extraordinarily dramatic to make the news.

So don't be fooled into thinking that violence is not occurring in your neighborhood just because it doesn't show up in the paper.

In virtually every neighborhood, people are dying by their own hand, often with a firearm. In 1992, suicides outnumbered homicides 21 to 16. Nine suicides have occurred already in 1993, one of them claiming a high-school student.

Domestic violence usually goes unreported in the news media until one of those involved — invariably the woman — winds up dead. But heads are being smashed, necks choked, lips busted every night of the week all over the city.

Shootings are an almost daily occurrence. Ask anyone who works in an emergency room.

As a reporter, I'm frustrated that I can't always tell you about each violent happening. But I must deal with the realities of newspaper space, competing news and deadlines.

One consolation is that I've not yet been asked to do a "Murder Roundup." May that day never come.

Oct. 15, 1993

Cops don't look at weekends as you probably do

Saturday was cold and rainy. How many calls for service do you think the Tallahassee Police Department received?

Maybe 20? Or 150? Or as many as 200? (Those were some of the answers from co-workers and friends.)

Try 619.

And that was a slow day.

"Most weekends we get between 800 and 900 calls a day," said Police Chief Tom Coe. "During our peak times, like during the Miami (vs. Florida State) football weekend, we can get more than 1,000."

Calls for service include everything from a complaint about a barking dog to a murder. In each case, an officer is sent out or takes a report over the phone.

During the past 10 years, the number of patrol officers has grown by 50 percent, to 175. And the number of calls has increased by nearly 250 percent, to 300,000.

In various combinations over a Saturday's 24 hours, 78 officers answered those 619 calls. Most of them weren't serious enough to warrant a report. Officers may have gone to a neighborhood where gunshots were heard, but nobody was around when they got there. Or they may have helped an elderly person who had fallen out of bed. Or calmed down a rowdy party.

But about a tenth of the calls required a report that ended up on the desk of the public-information officer Sunday morning.

If you thumbed through the stack of yellow reports, here's some of what you'd find:

- ♦ 21 reports of theft, burglary or robbery.
- ♦ Seven reports of battery, including domestic.
- ♦ Six arrests of people police were already looking for.
- ♦ Five trespass warnings.
- ♦ Four reports of criminal mischief (broken windows, convertible top cut).
- ♦ Four reports of drug-related arrests.
- ♦ Four reports of suspicious incidents (a man carrying a can of paint who lied about where he was going).
- ♦ Three reports of obscene or harassing phone calls.
- ♦ Two reports of disorderly conduct.
- ♦ Miscellaneous reports including a hit-and-run, loitering, prowling and violation of injunction.

Some of the reports were amusing, such as the stranger who was found sleeping in a motel room rented by someone else.

Other reports were pitiful, such as the store thief who knocked down an 86-year-old woman in a mall parking lot as he was trying to flee. They arrested someone in that case.

At least one report made your skin crawl.

A 19-year-old FSU student opened her door around 8:30 p.m. to find a man with his pants pulled down and masturbating. After a struggle, she managed to close the door. When her roommate looked out the peephole, however, she saw that the man had gone right on to the apartment across from them.

He was gone by the time police arrived.

Another Saturday approaches. Maybe it will be a slow day, just another 600 calls or so.

Feb. 4, 1994

An invisible sign declares: Women, beware

The man drove down the canopied trail on what is to become the Phipps-Overstreet-Maclay Greenway, talking about how people will soon be able to jog or hike 5 miles from Lake Hall to Lake Jackson through the wilderness.

Stopping the car, he gestured toward pristine Lake Overstreet, sighed deeply and then listened to the quiet stillness of the lake and woods.

Yes, this is great, the woman with him agreed.

"But you know," she added, "women will never be able to come here alone."

The man looked startled, then grew thoughtful. "I never thought about that."

When a woman can't even walk to work in broad daylight without a man grabbing her from behind and fondling her — which happened to a Tallahassee woman this week — it's doubtful that many women will hike alone in the woods.

There might as well be a posted sign near large parks or trail heads: "Women alone not allowed."

No one says this, of course. And it's not as if a lone man couldn't also be the target of a crime. But that doesn't seem to stop men from venturing outside by themselves the way it does women.

Take the St. Marks Trail. In September, a woman riding her bike along the trail by herself was raped and severely beaten.

Numerous conversations with women make it clear: The number of solo female riders on the trail has dropped dramatically.

Says one woman, who used to ride the trail by herself about every six weeks: "I think it's implanted in people's minds now that it's easy to pick women off the trail. They might think: That guy was slow, he got caught, but someone else a little less angry and a little more patient could get away with it."

Park supervisors and police say there's little they can do to make large tracts of land totally safe, but there is a growing awareness that smaller parks can be designed to discourage crime.

Officer Jeff Rioux with the Tallahassee Police Department's Crime Prevention Unit has been working with planners the past few years on a concept called Crime Prevention Through Environmental Design. For parks, that can include building a parking lot that is visible from all areas of the park, to reduce the chance of someone breaking into your car. Or taking down the brick screen around bathrooms to allow people to see who's going in and coming out.

In making suggestions, Rioux said, he always uses what he calls the mother/daughter rule — since men are often the ones designing things, and they can overlook certain safety features.

"If you build something that will be safe for (mothers and daughters), then you're probably doing the right thing," Rioux said. "If it's not, then I say, 'Let's try this one again.'"

It's a start. But hiking trails through woods, no matter how safe the rest of the park, will still seem dangerous to women.

Barring the creation of a park where men aren't allowed (wouldn't that be something!), it's a rare woman who'll be found alone in the woods, surrounded by silence, lost in her own thoughts.

April 1, 1994

A day with David was even better than 'Lion King'

It began while we were eating French toast for breakfast.

David wanted me to read a page from his new book about American Indians. The Northeast tribe who dried salmon by stringing them up between poles had captured his imagination.

"Why don't we go to the library and get more books about Indians?" I asked.

His coffee-bean eyes gleamed with pleasure, and he crooned, "Yeaaaaah."

I didn't tell him about the invitation from our neighbors to see "The Lion King." Spending several hours of unscheduled time with David was more appealing.

Since he started kindergarten, our conversations in the morning have consisted primarily of my bellowing, "Get your shoes on — now!" a couple of hundred times.

This day, I vowed not to use the words "Hurry up" the entire time.

On the way to the library, David asked, "Mommy, can we go to the Capitol?" Tall buildings, another one of his passions.

"Sure, if it's open, we can go."

We zipped through the library in 20 minutes, and then started our hike to the Capitol.

It took us a while. We stopped at the renovated E. Peck Green Park and checked out the new black and gold water fountain. Then, after we passed the Florida League of Cities office, David dropped to his knees to peer down a sewer grate.

As he checked out the ladder that led to the underground pipe, I smelled something minty and sweet. Behind me was a cluster of rosemary, its stems filled with sharp, spindly needles. I snapped one off and put it to David's nose.

"Mmmmmm. I love it. Let's keep it, Mommy," he said, and I slipped it into the pocket of my T-shirt.

Crossing College Avenue, we saw construction workers maneuvering huge cranes and churning up concrete on the site of the new parking garage behind City Hall. Clenching a wire fence, we watched the workers in silence. Suddenly, the sun burst through a dark cloud overhead, making the red clay on the construction site a bright orange.

Luckily, the Capitol was open.

Getting off on the 22nd floor, David rushed over to the window. Could we really see all the way to Georgia?

He stood up on the ledge, his arm wrapped around my neck, my arm encircling his waist.

"I want to live in Tallahassee my *whole* life," he informed me.

I pointed out the train moving along the overpass on Apalachee Parkway, and his mouth dropped open. We were late getting back to the elevator with the other visitors.

As we were stepping off on the fifth floor, David dropped to his knees and pressed his nose to the floor, trying to see down the crack between the elevator and the floor. "I guess you'll never know what's there unless you look for yourself," said one older gentleman.

David was attentive during the tour of the legislative chambers, but by the time he got to the Old Capitol, his feet were dragging.

He perked up, however, when I bought him an arrow-head for 50 cents. All the way back to the car, he jabbed the glassy, black stone into the air.

Back at home, David packed for an overnight stay at his friend's. When he was out the door a few minutes later, I closed the blinds and lay across the bed, ready for a nap.

As I drifted off to sleep, I inhaled a sweet, minty smell. The rosemary needle, crushed and giving off fragrance, still clung to the inside of my T-shirt pocket.

Sept. 27, 1994

A pair of dashing pirates ready to take on the world

The discussion of what to be for Halloween started in early September.

"Mom, what do *you* think I should be?" my 6-year-old asked.

"I don't know, David, what sounds good?"

"I think maybe a pirate."

Every time we passed Hancock Fabrics, he bugged me to go in. It had become a tradition for me to make his costume.

His first Halloween I sewed a clown's outfit, multi-colored stripes on one side, polka dots on the other, with a yellow collar.

The next year I spent agonizing hours fitting together a 42-piece stegosaurus costume, complete with tail and spikes down the head and back. Granted, he looked adorable, but it's an experience I didn't want to repeat.

A pirate costume would be a breeze.

But within days he had another idea: Why not buy one?

I hemmed and hawed. I never, ever had a store-bought costume when I was a kid. My mother always indicated that they were flimsy, unimaginative, not *authentic*.

But 19 days before Halloween, David gave me an ultimatum: We either went to the fabric store that night, or he was ready to plunk down his money at Toys-R-Us. Instead, I rummaged through my closet trying to come up with a good pirate's costume. It didn't take long.

Within minutes he was wearing a black vest, black pants and a red sash around his waist. He stood in front of the mirror, tilting his chin from side to side.

"Mmmmm, I don't think so," he said.

We added a red bandana and a gold loop earring.

He still wasn't convinced.

Then I did something I hadn't planned.

"Maybe I'll be a pirate for Halloween, too," I suggested tentatively.

I held my breath. Would this be appealing to a 6-year-old boy?

David stood still for a second, then looked up at me with his eyes shining. "Yeah! Great!"

My heart grew two sizes.

Shortly, I, too, was dressed all in black, a red sash around my waist, my hair tucked into a bandana. We stood in front of the mirror together. David was all grins. I couldn't wipe the smirk off my face either.

We were *dashing*.

The next day I bought us matching plastic swords, eye patches and makeup for beards and scars. I couldn't tell who was more excited when I brought them home, him or me. I secretly kept my fingers crossed that nobody would tease him and cause him to suddenly back out. Who ever heard of a woman pirate?

But last week, in Rubyfruit Books, I noticed the book: "Bold in Her Britches: Women Pirates Across the Ages," by Jo Stanley.

David was with me. What luck.

"Look, David, here's a book on women pirates."

"Cool. Can we get it?"

The $26 price tag was a little steep, but I showed him the cover with a painting of a woman pirate dressed in a cape. Whether it made any difference to him, I don't know. But I suddenly felt legitimate.

And now, today, after two months' anticipation, Halloween is here. We're ready, swords poised, to take on the world.

And maybe, David suggested one night recently as he was lying in bed, we could be pirates again next year.

"We could keep our costumes special all year long," he said as he turned on his side and shut his eyes.

We sure could, li'l mate.

We sure could.

Oct. 31, 1995

A closer look showed this bear was very Special

David saw it first.

To me, the bunched-up reddish material looked like someone's cast-off sweater lying by the side of the road.

But David had to take a closer look. He immediately braked his bike, snapped his kickstand down and rushed over to the soggy mess. I didn't want him to even touch it, but before the words were out of my mouth, he had picked it up.

I watched my 6-year-old son's face crumple.

What he held up was not a sweater, but the remains of a nearly decapitated teddy bear.

"I don't believe someone would just leave it here to *die*!" David choked out, his eyes welling up with tears.

His reaction surprised me. Empathy is one of those things parents try to impart to children, but not always successfully.

David and I had had several discussions about a chubby boy at school whom all the kids teased. When I picked David up from school one day recently, I found out just how ugly it had become. Unbeknownst to the teachers, a child had posted a sign on the bulletin board stating that the following list of kids hated this boy.

David's name was on it.

"How would you like it if someone did that to you?" I had asked him, trying to swallow my horror. "Remember when you were new and the big kids picked on you?"

His response had been noncommittal and, I thought, heartless. And now here he was crying over an inanimate object.

"What should we do with it?" he asked me, holding the teddy bear up by the arms.

"Why don't you just leave it there?" I responded.

"No," he sniffed. "I want to keep it, even though it looks like this."

I agreed to carry it home on my handlebars. I touched it as little as possible, grabbing it around the neck with my thumb. The smell of grease and mildew wafted up my nose.

At home, we spread the teddy bear out on the carport to assess the damage. One side of the face, including an eye and an ear, was gone. The neck was connected to the body by one tiny piece of material. The stuffing for the head was nonexistent.

"First we'll dry it out," I said finally, "then we'll sew it back up and then we'll wash it."

I was softening. The teddy bear did look awfully pathetic.

A few minutes later, while we were washing the mildew smell off our hands, I suggested we give the teddy bear a name.

"What about Red?" I said. "After all, you don't see many red teddy bears."

David shook his head, his eyes getting watery again. After a moment's thought, his face suddenly brightened.

"Special," he said, looking up at me enthusiastically. "We can call him Special. I'm going to love him more than any of my other stuffed animals."

At that moment, I felt certain that someday he would look upon that chubby boy at school with similarly compassionate eyes.

Over the next few days we put Special back together, doing cosmetic surgery on his ear, forehead and neck. A black button became his second eye. On the back of his head we sewed a heart patch, embroidered with his name and the date we found him.

"I knew we could do it," David said as we neared completion.

As I looked at Special — who, despite my best efforts, had ears that stuck way out, a neck that wobbled and a lingering smell — I reminded David that he would never look like other teddy bears. David thought about that.

"Well," he said finally, flipping up one hand and shrugging, "we could call him Different."

Jan. 23, 1996

Who cares about sports? Now I do

I don't read the sports page.

Ever.

But Wednesday morning, I couldn't get to the newspaper fast enough. Even though I had seen the U.S. women's gymnastics team win the gold the night before, I wanted to read about it again in the paper.

I was barely in the door at work when I heard co-workers talking about it, too. I joined in immediately.

This kind of "How about them 'Noles!" conversation is alien to me. Most times I think sports — especially football — is overrated. Who cares how many times some guy carries a ball across a goal line?

And that's just it. It will always be a guy. What would it take to make millions of people in the world watch a *woman* do *anything*, I often wondered.

Well, I found out Tuesday night.

I was glued to the tube. So was a woman I work with who never reads the sports pages, either.

For the first time, I felt included in a sport viscerally. It was Kerri Strug, a woman, who dug down deep, pulled out her best and had the world on its feet.

It's not the first time women have excelled in sports. But there was something special about the whole group of them, giving it their all, that got through to me.

The next day, at the gas station, I couldn't help it.

"Did you see the women's gymnastics final last night?" I asked the attendant.

He hadn't, so I repeated the whole last scene to him. Oh, now he remembered. Someone else had told him about it.

"That must have been something," he said.

Yeah, I thought, getting into my car, what *about* them gals!

July 26, 1996

A football game turns into a war when...

There it was in 4-inch type: WAR!

(Almost as large as the headline when the Gulf War started.)

I cringed.

For the past several weeks, I had stayed out of the football fever surrounding the Florida State-Florida game. Personally, I have no interest in football. Zip.

But let other people have their fun, I thought. I would just ignore all the extravagant *Democrat* coverage.

But with a headline like that on the morning of the game, I couldn't ignore it. With a headline like that, I felt compelled to speak out.

I thought about people the world over who are experiencing or have experienced real war. People in Zaire. People in Bosnia. People in our own hometown who have served in Korea, Vietnam or World War II.

I thought about mothers saying tearful goodbyes to sons. About bodies being blown to bits. About children crouching in bombed-out buildings.

This headline was a cruel joke.

Then I started thinking about money. News reporters are always told: Follow the money, that's where the power is. So we track the money and ask the hard questions: Is the money being spent wisely? Are officials being held accountable?

But are we using our own resources wisely?

I hope none of my sports co-workers take personal offense here. I know they work hard and are excellent at what they do. But the question of priorities still needs to be asked.

All I know is that a paper that boasts special section after special section on sports can't even afford, here in the Bible Belt, one full-time religion reporter.

Granted, we now have regular correspondents who write about religion — which we didn't have in the past — but, to me, it's slow going.

Values. It all comes down to values. Ours and our readers'.

Sports sells, I'm told. Readers want it. They bought up every last copy of the *Democrat* following the Big Game.

But I ask: Wouldn't those papers have sold anyway, without the war-mentality headlines?

And how do we know religion won't sell? It's never been given the resources that sports has.

Don't get me wrong: I think the *Democrat* does a lot of positive things. We cover everything from community problems like teenage pregnancy to everyday concerns like school-bus problems.

And, yes, we produce award-winning sports coverage.

But let's rein it in.

Maybe we can take some advice from the book, "Unplug the Christmas Machine," by Jo Robinson and Jean Coppock Staeheli.

There's nothing wrong with gift-giving, the authors say. It's fun to eat special foods, go to parties, decorate your house.

But what happens when holiday mania gets out of hand? Too much commercialism dampens the spirit.

So they advise taking stock: What's important here? What can go by the wayside? How can we spend money in ways that reflect our true values?

As a community, as a newspaper, we can do this with football. We can "unplug the Seminole Machine." Bring it back down to size.

After all, it's not a war.

It's just a game.

Dec. 8, 1996

Digest these tales from a trip to the Bog of the Bug-Eating Plants

When I was going to grade school, there were no such things as field trips. The nuns at St. Domitilla in Hillside, Ill., were pros at teaching us English and math, but we never did anything *hands-on*.

Once, in first grade, we went to the edge of the parking lot and picked out fall leaves for an art project. The sky was a strange green color, and the wind whipped around my blue plaid jumper and gray Hush Puppies. Some leaves, already a dull brown, rattled across the asphalt; others were still blotched with red and yellow. I reached out and grabbed one.

That's it.

It was with particular delight, then, that I went with my 8-year-old son, David, on a recent field trip to a bog.

Bring an old pair of shoes you don't care about, said the teachers at Full Flower, a small, alternative school off Mahan Drive.

Good advice, because we were going to get down and *dirty*.

On the way there, David and two other boys filled me in on what we were going to see: carnivorous plants.

They could hardly contain themselves.

"They eat insects!" I learned.

"And they *stink* when you open them up."

"And bugs get caught and they can't get out and they just *dissolve!*"

Oh, yum.

Carnivorous plants grow in areas with little or no nitrogen and need the decaying insects for nutrients.

The boys expected to see at least three plants that day:

- ♦ Pitcher plants. These narrow ice-cream-cone-shaped plants have thick, bristly hair inside and fill with water when it rains. Insects, attracted by the sweet smell, are first trapped by the hairs, then slide down the tube and drown.
- ♦ Sundews. The long, spindly leaves of this plant are covered with clear, sticky droplets. When insects alight near them, they get stuck. The leaves then curl up around the bug and kill it.
- ♦ Venus flytraps (destined to be the kids' favorite). This clam-shaped plant has sharp, teeth-like edges. If an insect gets near — chomp! — it snaps shut and feasts on that little delicacy for about two weeks. (The kids were told they could dig up the plants since they aren't native to Florida and are considered "exotic.")

When we arrived at the bog, just west of Hosford, the boys could barely wait until the van had stopped before they were out the door and plunging one foot and then the other into the mud.

It took them about two seconds to find the plants.

"It's got two of my fingers!" yelled Jourdan Joly as he crouched near a Venus flytrap.

They fanned out over the roadside area like locusts, buzzing here and there, trying to take all of it in as fast as they could.

"What's a sundew? I want to see a sundew," said Alex Rathavon, her eyes scanning the ground from side to side as she waded in the water.

Others were scattered around, competing with each other to find the best Venus flytrap. "That's the most pretty one," said David Canter, pushing aside the other kids. "I want to get that one."

Orien Canter darted ahead of the others, trying to be the first to find something new. "This is, like, the *best* place," he said.

When their teacher, Michael Ray, took out his knife, the kids stopped their individual explorations and rushed to his side. Holding a pitcher plant in one hand, he ran the knife through the plant from top to bottom. As he peeled apart the base, he looked up, his nose wrinkled in disgust. Those decaying bugs can sure smell nasty.

But the students loved it.

"Ooooh, yuck! It stinks," they'd say, after insisting they get a whiff.

For the next hour, they continued to slog through the bog, filling their pots with Venus flytraps.

"Mine won't even fit in this bucket," moaned Patrick Chanton.

On the way home, the boys jabbered about their plants: whose was the biggest, whose had the most flytraps, whose plant had been fed which bug.

"Don't water them with anything but distilled water — it'll kill them," Orien said solemnly. The designated class expert on the plants, he had been gathering information for weeks from the Internet and the library.

The other boys agreed. Nothing but the best for their plants.

For days afterward, David fawned over his Venus flytrap, misting it, bringing it outside for sunshine and feeding it a grasshopper. "I always wanted one of these," he'd gush.

Our shoes are still caked in mud. And though we soaked our socks in a bucket with bleach for more than a week, they still aren't clean.

But I like to think that even Sister Patrice would have thought it was worth it. Dirt and all.

Oct. 21, 1997

See Noah trot!
See Mom run!

Standing in line at Walgreen's last week, I noticed a woman with her two small children standing behind me. Someone asked her how old her daughter was.

"Oh, she just turned 2," the woman answered.

I looked down at the toddler calmly holding her mother's hand. Two, I thought.

Amazing.

I wouldn't dare bring *my* almost-2-year-old to a drugstore.

He'd run down the aisles, pull things off the shelf, shriek uproariously when things fell to the floor and then zip over to the cash register or charge through the door marked "Employees Only."

And me — I'd be doing the Noah Trot.

"Noah! Stop! Noah! Come here!" I'd be yelling, prancing after him with hands outstretched and bent slightly at the waist so that if I *did* catch up with him, I *might* be able to scoop him up in my arms.

But, of course, that wouldn't work either. He'd only kick and scream and wiggle, wiggle, wiggle until I put him down.

And then he'd be off again.

Is it payback for never putting him in a playpen? Has my let-the-child-make-as-many-decisions-as-possible approach to parenthood gone too far?

Whatever the case, I don't take him out in public much.

I made that mistake about a month ago when I went to the Leon County Public Library. Even with all the kids who troop through that institution, I heard sighs of relief when we finally walked out the door.

He had been going full-throttle inside. Down this aisle. Up on that chair — bang! bang! bang! on the computer. Whooosh! Up the steps. Books fell, videos flew. Even his 8-year-old brother, David, was exasperated.

"Mo-om! Get him! Get him!"

OK, so my kid won't behave indoors. Outdoors should be better.

Should be.

I took him to Chaires Elementary School one recent Saturday morning. The playground there — if you've never been — is a kid's paradise. Tons of wooden structures to climb, wooden bridges to cross, tiny spaces to crawl in.

Noah loved it. For about 10 minutes. Even with David saying, "Come here, Noah, let's go here," he wasn't interested.

He wanted to explore. By himself.

Trot, trot, trot, down to the farthest reaches of the field. Then he's scrambling up the steps to the school. He shrieks and the hallways echo. He looks up in wonder. "Ooooooh! Oooooooh!" he starts yelling, running down the corridor and listening to the sound reverberate. Then he spies a bus at the other end of the school. He's off.

Getting him back into the car, of course, is a chore. Kick. Scream. Arch back.

I'm exhausted. I'm always exhausted.

Normal, say the childhood experts. Two-year-olds are impulsive and you have to watch them every minute.

I guess. But when I ask my sister, who has three kids, if any of hers were like Noah, she hesitates, "Well, no. My kids didn't run off much. But I've known kids like that."

You should be so lucky.

The only thing that keeps me going is thinking, "This, too, shall pass." By his third birthday, surely, things will be better. I try to visualize this when I'm collapsed on the couch, arm slung over my eyes, and murmuring softly, "One more year, one more year," to the rhythm of the Little Red Caboose.

Sighing, I resolve to keep my doors securely closed for the whole next year. To keep him out of stores. To *never* take him to the library.

Instead, I'm resigned to perfecting the Noah Trot. One, two, three, run-run, shout! shout! One, two, three, shout!

"Noah! Stop! Noah! Come here!"

Date unknown

Galloping days have just begun for this parent

A couple of years ago, I couldn't take Noah anywhere in public. My then 2-year-old son would fling books off the shelf in the library, dash behind the checkout counter in stores and run to the farthest end of any park or field.

In a column titled "Trotting After Noah," I wrote that surely by the time he was 3 we'd be past this stage.

Well, Noah is now 4 and, yes, my trotting days are over. My galloping days, however, have just begun.

Consider a recent morning I spent at Lake Ella with Noah and my 10-year-old son, David. We were walking around the lake when Noah suddenly slumped his shoulders forward, dropped his head to his chest and began walking in the opposite direction. I waited for him to turn around — if only to see whether I was looking.

Not a chance.

I started walking after him, still anticipating that look over the shoulder. When it didn't come, I picked up my pace.

"Noah!" I yelled. "Noah!"

He sped up. Although he didn't run out into the street, I began to panic that I would lose sight of him. One kind woman tried to stop him but he wiggled out of her hands and broke into a dead run.

By now I was racing down the sidewalk. Perfect strangers were yelling with me — "Noah! Noah! Stop!" — and trying to catch him.

He was in full throttle.

Finally, a friend of mine who happened to be at the lake scooped him up and held him. Trying to avoid the eyes of onlookers, I carried the kicking and screaming child to the car.

Out of breath, with sweat dripping down my neck, I blew up as soon as the car door was shut.

"Don't you ever run away from me like that again!" I said, glaring at him in the rearview mirror.

It was only after I had come home, sent Noah to his room and puffed through a half-hour Jane Fonda tape that my rage began to subside.

I've learned that Noah's activeness — to say nothing of this persistence — is not a developmental phase. It's part of his personality.

One child psychologist said that Noah wasn't hyperactive, but that we could count on him to push the limits all of his childhood.

"He'll always be like that to some degree," she said.

Some might call him a "difficult" child. One generous author, who wrote about such children, uses the word "spirited."

Whatever the case, normal disciplinary techniques don't work with him. At least not for long.

Much of the time we feel inadequate and embarrassed as parents. Surely if we were more "consistent" (you have no idea how many times people have used that word with us), he wouldn't be this way.

Luckily, Noah is a charmer. The same kid who will ignore my demands to come back into the house or to put down that stick will make your heart melt with one of his dimpled smiles. And he's the most affectionate child I've ever known.

"Hi!" he'll yell exuberantly to a stranger walking down the street. "I want to give you a hug!"

He also has a unique sense of humor. Recently he changed his name to David, the same as his older brother's. "I'm David 2," he'll say with a straight face to everyone he encounters. Then he'll break into a grin and chuckle.

And he doesn't miss a trick. "Are we going to a meeting?" he asked one day.

"No," I replied. "Why would you think that?"

"Because you have that shirt on."

Three months ago I had worn the shirt to a school meeting.

The bottom line is that, underneath the anger Noah often provokes in me, I admire the little rascal. He's got guts. Chutzpah. A no-holds-barred approach to life.

I just hope I can remember that the next time I'm galloping around Lake Ella.

July 20, 1999

Time chatting in park adds grace to life

In "Ordinary Grace," author Kathleen Brehoney relays story after story of people being kind. Some are as time-limited as the teen who helps a boy with no arms or legs up a mountain. Others require more commitment: One woman donates a kidney to someone she barely knows.

But whether the gesture is large or small, Brehoney maintains that all of us are surrounded by people who, by their spontaneous acts of giving, fill our lives with grace.

One such woman lives in my neighborhood in Indian Head Acres. She'd die of embarrassment if I mentioned her by name, so I'll just call her Miz Generous, or Miz G for short.

If you live anywhere around Koucky Park — especially if you own a dog — you know which woman I mean. Every afternoon you'll find her sitting on the bench, dressed in her trademark khaki pants, plaid shirt and fisherman's hat, her pockets stuffed with dog biscuits.

As people wander by, she slips the dogs a treat and converses with the owner about everything from Emily Dickinson to the latest guest on "Oprah." The retired educator reminds the kids when mulberries are in season and holds on to their special toys when they rush home to poop.

My 11-year-old son has had long discussions with her about who-knows-what, his leg kicking the dust below the bench, their voices rising and falling, breaking into laughter. My 4-year-old son has wrapped his arms around her neck and exclaimed, "I love to hug people I like!"

Patting his arm, she softly replies, "Me, too."

She has left gifts on our doorstop: tomatoes, oranges, cracked pecans, pink camellias. When my son expresses an interest in geology and archaeology, she brings him an arrowhead and a slice of petrified wood. She's introduced me to the writing of Nicaraguan poet Daisy Zamora and the music of violinist Leila Josefowic. She brings treats for the kids every birthday, Halloween and Christmas.

But Miz G's greatest gift is time. While many of us in the neighborhood are scurrying to and fro, squeezing in our late-afternoon walk between work and dinner, barely able to stop and say hello, she acts as if she has all the time in the world. She's always ready to sit a spell. Chat about the day and our lives. Pick up threads of conversations we may have begun three weeks ago. If we get itchy to move on, she'll fix her keen eyes on us for several seconds and then sigh.

"OK, go, go," she'll say, waving her hand.

We're losing the art of conversation, she told me recently as we sat together on the bench. Too many other distractions.

I had to agree. Getting anybody's attention for more than a few brief moments is rare.

That's why Miz G is so special to me. I've never told her so directly. But I've thought it often as I've watched the sun set in the park, the trees filling with golden light, the dogs at our feet. Even our pauses are full of grace.

May 2, 2000

The tyranny of birthday parties

Every time I go to the mailbox and pull out a 3-by-5 envelope, especially if I can see the outline of a Dalmatian or Pokemon, I cringe:

Another birthday invitation.

Before either of my two boys can see it, I dump it into the trash. You might call me a scrooge, but really, how many of these can a sensible person take?

One birthday party can be fun. Maybe two, possibly even three. But if you're like Terry and me, or many other parents, your entire weekend can be scheduled around birthday parties if you're not careful. One recent Sunday, our 11-year-old son scurried from one neighborhood party to the next without so much as a gulp of air in between. (The older they get, the less that trash-dumping technique works.)

And then there's the gluttony. Mounds and mounds of presents. Tons of sugar. And children go home with a bag of little toys they can add to their truckload of party favors from previous parties.

Our children need this?

I don't think so. In fact, parents would be doing their kids a favor if they started a birthday party boycott. Or at least put a yearly cap on the number of parties they can attend — say, four.

We'd be showing them restraint. Discipline. Disdain for wanton materialism. Besides, we could spend our Saturday afternoons in the hammock instead of rushing to Toys "R" Us, scrounging around for wrapping paper and then sitting through two hours of kid bedlam.

The biggest problem is that many parents — especially middle- and upper-class — throw their kids a party *every year*. And not your cheap, pin-the-tail-on-the-donkey ones in the back yard. Parents often rent space at places like Chuck E. Cheese or the Fun Station, or they pay a clown, a horse or a magician to entertain our already over-stimulated kids.

The first birthday party I ever had was when I was 16, and I turned out OK. (At least I haven't had to join an Adult Children Who Had No Kid Birthday Parties support group.)

One brave woman I know hasn't given her daughter a birthday party yet — and the girl is 7!

"N-n-n-not *one* party?" I stammered when she told me this one recent morning.

"Nope," she replied.

I think she deserves a "Mommy with Guts" award, don't you?

I haven't dared go that far yet. Both our sons have had birthday parties, some of which I actually enjoyed. But they don't get one every year. Last year, for example, Terry and I planned to throw Noah a party when he turned 4. But as the time drew near, we felt exhausted just thinking about it. One night she looked at me with bloodshot eyes and said, "Let's just skip it."

And we did. We made cupcakes for his preschool friends, turned up at snack time to pass them out and called it a day. Noah, who got to wear a paper crown all day, was delighted.

If you like giving parties — and I've met parents who actually do — don't let my rantings stop you. But if, like me, you find them tedious, join the boycott. You don't have to go to cold turkey. Maybe you'll cut down to a party every other year. Or maybe, like one mom I know, you can put a "No gifts" line in your invitation. You might even decide to skip the party favors or give them to needy children.

Start somewhere. It's all a part of becoming a Parent for a Saner Birthday World.

May 30, 2000

Between tears and rocket lectures, a nice family dinner

Family dinners, some experts say, can help children learn manners, encourage communication and even — get this — help improve test scores! I'm sure you've heard the stories. We had one on the manners connection is this section just last week.

These reports just make me sigh. I've been doing family dinners for more than seven years, and guess what?

My kids are still animals.

No matter how many times I've said, "Small bites, David, small bites," my 11-year-old wolfs down food so fast that even the word "inhale" doesn't do him justice. My 5-year-old just *has* to bang his silverware on the table, against his glass or across his brother's arm. They fight over where they sit, who has what glass and who gets the last bite of cheese/bread/applesauce.

And tears. What is it about the dinner hour that brings such powerful emotions to the surface? Even when I think I've managed the timing perfectly — giving them an afternoon snack, letting them watch a bit of TV, kindly asking them to wash their hands — one or the other often falls apart just as we're sitting down at the table.

Even something as simple as giving thanks turns into a battle of wills. David refuses to hold Noah's hand. "They're gross!" he'll exclaim, pulling his hand away. At Terry's and my insistence, he'll reluctantly put a finger on Noah's forearm.

Noah, for his part, takes *forever* to finish giving thanks.

"Are you done now?" Terry will ask him after he's given his 10th reason for gratitude.

"No, not yet," he'll reply. "I give thanks for. . . ."

David, meanwhile, is seething.

My biggest disappointment is Friday night. For us, as a Jewish family, that's the beginning of Sabbath. It's traditional to make Sabbath dinner special by using a tablecloth, getting out the good silverware, lighting candles, buying flowers and a special bread called challah, and having dessert. I do it all. Every week, when I see the table spread out so beautifully, I feel a special peace and joy inside.

Until we sit down.

The kids fight over who lights the candles, who starts the prayer over the wine, who picks out the special Sabbath song. I threaten to eat in another room. Noah pokes David in the stomach.

More than once, Terry has looked at me and asked, "Why is it that we try to do these dinners?"

Got me.

But so far, I've refused to give them up. While dinner is often chaotic, we do have our moments. One night recently, after we had eaten, David treated us to a rocket lecture — diagrams and all. Another time, the boys sang a rendition of "All-Star" together, leaving Terry and me practically rolling on the floor. We've even managed to have good discussions about such things as school plays, camping trips, minority voting rights and the mechanics of a weather balloon.

And despite the poking and grumbling, my boys are not self-conscious giving thanks anywhere, anytime.

"Thanks, Mom, for making such a delicious dinner," Noah will say almost every night. He even, on occasion, says he loves his brother.

Now that's something you'd never hear eating dinner in front of the TV set.

July 25, 2000

Child-care workers deserve decent pay

In March, when thousands marched on the Capitol over affirmative action, I had an inspiration as I dropped off my child at Tallahassee Day School.

Wouldn't it be nice if some of that passion were focused on younger children? How about the injustice of preschool teachers' salaries?

That's enough to make your blood boil.

Most work for minimum wage. Almost none have health insurance. Few are compensated for professional training.

Yet some of these folks are the sages of our community.

I'll give you an example. When Noah was 3, he was a real charmer — but he had an intense personality. Putting him to sleep took hours. He dug in his heels about every little decision and tended to hit when angry or frustrated.

While we got a few pointers from psychologist-types, it was the advice I got from Julianna Stanton as we sat on the school's front porch that proved to be the most helpful.

She knew my child. She cared about him. And in addition to raising three sons, she has worked with hundreds of children over the past 20 years.

The woman everyone calls Miss Julianna knows her stuff. And she shares it for free.

That's why I think it's criminal that she and other child-care professionals are paid such a pittance.

Donna Spaulding, who works at Faith Baptist Child Development Center, said she's been able to stay in the field for the past 10 years only because her husband makes enough money for the family.

"If I was a single mother, or even a single person, I couldn't survive," she said.

Something is wrong with this picture. We know that the No. 1 indicator of a good child-care center is the quality of the teachers. But if they're not paid enough or given enough benefits, good teachers are hard to attract and keep. How many people do you know who'd work without insurance?

Raising child-care rates isn't an adequate option. If centers paid teachers what they're worth, the cost to parents would be exorbitant.

So I have another idea: Let's get noisy.

Just like the march on the Capitol to protest One Florida, we need a groundswell of support for the professionals who care for our children.

People would flock to Tallahassee by car, by bus, driving all night to get here. Hotels would be booked up. Demonstrators would carry signs: "Insurance for all child-care pros!" "Nothing less than $10 an hour!" "Stop wage-ism now!"

It's not that far-fetched. If we can have public education, Social Security and an interstate road system, we can make sure our child-care professionals are adequately paid.

So let's plan a march for next spring. We can join hands with those folks who are helping us form a village for our children. I'm even willing to take Noah out of his big-boy kindergarten class so he can be part of this historic movement.

Aug. 8, 2000

Guilt gets modern mothers nowhere

When a colleague of mine had a baby several months ago, I half-jokingly welcomed her to Guilt Land. As a modern mom, she won't be able to get away from it.

Put your kid in child care and continue to work. Guilt. *(How can I leave my baby with someone else?)*

Stay at home full time. Guilt. *(I'm not using my college education — what kind of example is that for the kids? And what if I end up divorced in a few years?)*

Work part time. Guilt. *(I'm not doing either one of these jobs justice.)*

Round and round we go. No matter which way we turn it, our stomach churns.

That's why I gobbled up a report recently released by Public Agenda, a nonpartisan public policy research organization.

The purpose of the study, "Necessary Compromises," was to see how parents, employers and children's advocates viewed child care today and what that might mean for public policy.

Some of the findings:

♦ Although most American women with children younger than 5 work outside the home, 70 percent of parents said it's best for the child if a parent is home full time.

♦ Parents and child advocates differ on public policy solutions. Parents want tax cuts to help them stay home; advocates want to raise child-care center standards.

♦ Parents distrust child-care centers. Sixty-three percent said "children could suffer physical or sexual abuse" in a typical center; only 12 percent of advocates felt that way. (Statistically, more children are abused at home. But parents' fears skyrocket when they hear stories such as those of the two child-care workers sentenced last week in Leon County for kicking, hitting and slapping children.)

♦ Few parents are judgmental — 87 percent said mothers who work are just as loving and committed to their children as those who stay at home. Almost all recognized that staying home full time was not an option for many.

Interesting findings. But my bellyache remains.

Although respondents talked about having a "parent" home full time, we all know they really mean "mother." There's a tiny movement of stay-at-home dads, but honestly: How many dads do you know agonizing about this? I bet you can name a dozen moms who are.

It's definitely a mom thing.

To me, it seems that moms look out at the crazy world of guns and drugs and back-talking kids and think: *I have to do something. I* should *be at home.*

Dads look at the same things and say: *Something's wrong.* She *should be at home.*

In the study, even the idea of both parents working different shifts wasn't seen as much of a solution — it ranked below having a baby sitter or a close relative watch the child.

The scariest part was that women seemed to agree that it's mostly their problem. They were asked to respond to this statement: "Nowadays, many mothers reduce their hours and responsibilities at work so they can be home when their children are young." Sixty-seven percent responded: "This is just how life works — it's a choice that *mothers* and their families make for themselves." (Emphasis mine.)

So what's the solution? I'm as bewildered as everybody else. I hate the idea of women returning to the home in droves. We've been there, done that. While it might have been better for kids, it made a lot of women nuts. Those who found themselves divorced at midlife were at a particular disadvantage — and still are.

On the other hand, I hate the idea of handing over children — particularly infants — to day-care centers, or even an at-home baby sitter. As many of the respondents in the study said, "No one loves your children like you do."

I've also witnessed — and experienced — the stressful life of the two-career family. And it's no pretty picture.

But somehow the responsibility for giving our kids a good start must be shared by all. We need more tax cuts and better child-care centers, more caregiving dads and better job alternatives.

Keeping moms trapped in Guilt Land is not the answer.

Aug. 29, 2000

Pass the popcorn when you have 'One Life to Live'

If I have to say the words out loud, I'll blush. So I'll put it in writing instead: I'm a soap opera watcher.

Now this might not seem like a big deal to some, but I run with a rather highbrow crowd. Most of my friends would rather listen to National Public Radio than turn on the tube. One even sports the bumper sticker "Kill Your Television." For our part, Terry and I limit our sons' TV to one hour a day and let them watch only PBS, the Discovery Channel or Animal Planet.

So why, then, after the kids are in bed, will you find us with the blinds closed, the lights dimmed, curled up in front of the TV watching taped episodes of "All My Children" and "One Life to Live"?

Call it a major weakness.

I never thought I'd succumb. Terry is a lifelong watcher, and when we got together 17 years ago I'd chide her: "How can you watch this stuff?"

I couldn't imagine how an otherwise intelligent woman could get anything out of these improbable story lines.

But after our first son was born, I was so tired at night that I'd find myself glancing at the screen. "Now who is he?" I'd ask. "Is she still in love with him? She's had how many husbands?"

Before I knew it, I was piecing the whole story together — and wanting to know what happened next.

Surely, I thought, this was a temporary lapse in judgment during early motherhood. Fat chance. More than a decade later, I'm still addicted. (Unbeknownst to most people, we even named our second son, Noah, after one of the characters on "All My Children.")

I've watched Erica Kane have at least four new loves, Jessica Buchanan go from a child to a woman and Todd Manning leave the show, come back, leave the show and come back again.

What, might you ask, keeps me coming back? Here's my best excuse: The story never ends.

In most aspects, soap operas don't resemble real life much. Once, just once, I'd like to see one of the characters holding a toilet bowl cleaner or wearing the same outfit twice.

But on another level, like real life, there's always tomorrow. Most movies have a way of wrapping up lives in a tidy package at the end. Love stories, in particular, are guilty of this. Whenever I see couples ride off into the sunset, I smirk, "Yeah, right. I'd like to see them after being married for five years, day in, day out. Wonder how passionate things would be then."

While soap opera stars might do all their emotional work dressed in designer clothes, you do get to see what happens after the honeymoon — and it's not always pretty. People change, new loves emerge, tragedies happen. Getting introduced to new characters in movies, or even new people every few years in a sitcom or drama series, isn't anywhere near as satisfying. I like viewing people over the long haul.

In addition, some of the best acting I've witnessed has been on soap operas — when Cassie lost a baby, when Vicki was diagnosed with breast cancer, when Todd wrestled with his dark side, when Erica's daughter had anorexia. Those up-close shots of emotion running through their faces were amazing.

Sound highbrow enough? If not, consider this: Pulitzer-Prize-winning author Toni Morrison watches soap operas, too. I can't tell you how relieved I was when I read that tidbit in the *New York Times Magazine* a number of years ago. My only complaint is that the article didn't tell me *which one.*

I also know an FSU religion professor who watches "All My Children." Lucky for us, she lives in our neighborhood. When, for some reason, our VCR doesn't record our soaps, we slink over to her house in the dead of the night to get her tape.

Then we're ready for our nightly ritual: Terry will make me popcorn sprinkled with nutritional yeast, I'll pour a glass of wine and we'll both settle in for a visit with our TV friends.

Oct. 3, 2000

Call now: Breast cancer waits for no one

A few years ago, the words "breast cancer" had little effect on me. I was like a teen-ager who couldn't imagine getting in a car accident.

Then a friend of mine got it.

A year later, another friend was diagnosed.

Just last month, a *third* friend got the dreaded biopsy report.

It took this third case to shake me out of denial. I started reading everything I could on the subject. I searched the web. I scoured the cancer section of bookstores. I found out what *ductal carcinoma in situ* is (cancerous changes within the milk ducts) and what the best anti-cancer foods are (flaxseed and broccoli, to name two).

When I heard about the American Cancer Society's program Tell-a-Friend — asking volunteers to call five women older than 40 to remind them to get regular mammograms — I didn't space out the calls as I might have a few years ago. I immediately started talking to family and friends.

I also jumped at the chance to see "Sisters of Courage," the photo exhibit on display this month at the Tallahassee Senior Center. Photojournalist Beth Reynolds from St. Petersburg took pictures of 26 survivors of breast and ovarian cancer from all over Florida and wrote a biograph-ical sketch on each one.

The black-and-white photos show women of all ages, races and backgrounds. There's a politician, a newspaper editor, a nurse, an artist and an aerobics instructor. One had just completed treatment. Two had survived more than 25 years. One had been diagnosed when she was eight months' pregnant.

In the bios, many expressed dismay over friends who were too scared to get a mammogram. Frances Mauer, 77, who pursued her lifelong interest in painting after her treatment, called these women "chicken."

Elena Canarago described what she thought had saved her life: a coupon for a free mammogram. At the time, she had no health insurance, had no family history of breast cancer and was only 40 years old. But when a friend gave her the coupon, she made an appointment.

I was particularly moved by the photo of Colleen Agresta, 37. Her husband had swooped her up in his arms as if he were going to carry her across the threshold after the wedding. Her head is thrown back in laughter; her two sons stand smiling at their side.

Humor, Agresta said, helped her recover. Her favor-ite story is about the day her family got her a "Hooters" T-shirt — and crossed out the "s."

These photos and stories engrossed me for a long time. I admired the women's courage, their wit, their honesty. I left knowing I had to do my part to spread the word. And you need to do yours.

October is Breast Cancer Awareness Month. Don't wait, as I did, until someone you love gets it before finding out about it. Do your self-exams. Get your mammograms. Encourage your loved ones to do the same.

The earlier the detection, the better the chance for survival.

In 15 years, I want to take black-and-white photos of my friends: Judith painting her wood snakes, Ellen doing yoga, Vicki in her herb and butterfly garden. Afterward, we'll talk about our lives. We'll look into each other's eyes. We'll laugh until the cows come home.

Oct. 10, 2000

Love and kindness can outshine the worst of hate

The images of Israel in the media right now are violent. Rock-throwing youth. Machine-toting soldiers. Bomb blasts and sirens.

The country seems awash in finger-pointing, hatred and anger. Peace feels like a distant dream.

But on the ground level, the people-to-people level, there are sparks of caring and love that cannot be squelched by overriding politics. Some Jews and Arabs are reaching out to one another. They share their grief, they cry and laugh together, they continue to meet.

I offer you four images of such interactions I discovered on the internet in email correspondence that has been forwarded to me. The incidents may seem insignificant compared to the avalanche of violence that has erupted. But sometimes, a simple act of love can burn longer than a bonfire of hate.

♦ Last spring, Eliyahu McLean, an Israeli, and Abu El Hawa, an Arab, worked together on several Jewish/Muslim events. Since the riots started, they hadn't talked.

Then they met on the street.

"As soon as he saw me, he burst out in tears, gave me a big hug and kissed me 10 times," Eliyahu wrote. "We held each other, mourning the awful turn of events which made our evening in Nebi Musa just two months ago seem like a dream."

Another Arab from Gaza told Eliyahu: "No matter what happens, we will always be friends."

♦ An Israeli woman is so sickened by the violence, she decides to buy a basket of treats for her Palestinian friend who lives in another town. Her 10-year-old daughter makes a cake in the shape of a heart.

"It was dumb, but I felt that I could somehow metaphorically neutralize the unspeakable hurt of all of this by drowning it in offerings of sweets," she wrote.

She gave the basket of jam, fruit and halva — a confection made of sesame seeds and honey — to her friend rather sheepishly, saying she wanted to "sweeten the bitterness of these days."

Her friend seemed to understand.

"She knew exactly where I was coming from, and we laughed together at the futility of that gesture and the rightness of it, too."

♦ For almost a year, 30 Muslim and Israeli children have been playing tennis together in the coastal town of Caesarea. The third- and fourth-graders are part of the Co-Existence Project, run by the Israel Tennis Center. Without the program, these kids would never have met.

In mid-October, when two Israelis were lynched in Ramallah, the tennis games stopped. The atmosphere seemed too volatile. Too dangerous.

But a week later, despite the continued violence between Israelis and Palestinians, the van carrying the Muslim children returned to the Caesarean tennis court.

"They're back!" the jubilant coach told a reporter from the Christian Science Monitor. "And the whole group all behaved exactly like usual. Kids live only in the present."

♦ In 1994, Itzhak Frankenthal's son was killed by a militant Islamic group. But instead of wanting revenge, Frankenthal, an Orthodox Jew, channeled his grief in another direction. He reached out to Arab parents who also had lost children. He started a group called Bereaved Parents' Circle, which today has about 100 members.

In mid-October, a group of Jewish parents met with Arab parents who had lost sons in the recent riots. Frankenthal shook hands with Farage Gnaim, whose son, Immad, had been killed. The father spoke about peace. Then Gnaim asked Frankenthal if he had a photograph of his son. Frankenthal took one out. Gnaim looked at it, brought it to his face and kissed it.

Nov. 14, 2000

Some of us fry latkes *and* hang Christmas stockings

When December rolls around, I fry potato latkes for Hanukkah and cook a turkey for Christmas. I light the menorah for eight days and hang stockings on the fireplace Christmas Eve.

I'm a tradition juggler.

Seven years ago, I decided to become a Jew. My life partner is Jewish, and we were raising our boys in her faith — but, more important, I had fallen madly in love with the religion. Since making my decision, I've tried to downshift during the Christmas season, minimizing the Christian aspects and emphasizing the Jewish ones.

But it ain't easy.

Christmas is in my blood, the memories still binding me to my family of origin and the larger society. I find myself humming Christmas carols, gazing longingly at decorations and almost weeping at the smell of a Fraser fir. On Christmas Eve, I yearn to be with my parents and sisters.

Although every year I let more and more of it go, I still hang on to some things.

I'm not alone. I've known a Catholic who became a Jew, a Jew who became a Mormon, a Christian who became a Buddhist and a Baptist who became a Rastafarian. Talk to any religious group and you'll find these folks — people who grew up in one tradition and converted to another.

Establishing family traditions — or passing them on — is a challenge. We're forced to be creative.

I let go of the Christmas tree about six years ago. We don't sing Christmas carols any more. We spend less and less on Christmas presents.

But we do hang up stockings. (My mother needlepointed and hand-stitched one for each of my two boys — how could I keep them in the closet?) We leave a cookie out for Santa Claus. On Christmas Day, I have a big potluck dinner at my house. I cook the turkey so I can still have the smell of boiling celery and onions (used for the dressing) as I did while I was growing up.

For Hanukkah, we light candles every night, say the blessing, sing songs, tell stories and play with the dreidel, a four-sided top marked with Hebrew letters and used in a game of chance. At least one night I make latkes, the potato pancakes that are traditionally served during this period.

Since Hanukkah is a minor Jewish holiday that's not even mentioned in the Torah, we downplay the gift part. Instead, we've started a tradition of giving each other only two presents each during the eight-day festival — and they have to be something you made or something you want to do for the other person. Last year David gave Terry and me five pancake breakfasts in bed — three of which we actually cashed in on. I've given them a walk down the creek or a canoe trip on the Wakulla River.

My compromises aren't perfect. I still feel embarassed to tell my Jewish friends I have Christmas dinner at my house. I don't mention my Jewish observances to my mother. To avoid conflict, we just never plan a visit around this time.

But somehow I think God appreciates my efforts. In my morning prayers I always thank the Holy One for "making me according to Your will." I believe God loves this mixed-up daughter.

Dec. 19, 2000

Her word around the house is going to the dogs

Don't you love it when your word carries weight? When people respect your opinions? When your authority goes unquestioned?

Me, too. I just wish it happened more often at my house.

Several months ago, Terry asked me whether we could get a Jack Russell terrier she had fallen in love with. She knew a man who was moving out of town and couldn't take the dog with him.

"No," I said. End of discussion. A few months earlier we had gotten a dog, Ralph, which was already a stretch for me. I didn't grow up with dogs and am not particularly fond of them. I got Ralph mostly for our two boys, although I have to admit that as dogs go, he's the best — has short hair, keeps tongue in mouth, seldom barks and has the sweetest face you've ever laid eyes on.

When Terry asked me about the Jack Russell again a few months later, I looked at her quizzically. Was she serious?

"AB-so-LUTE-ly not!" I said. I couldn't believe she was even *asking*.

A month ago, a breathless Terry called me at work. "Well, I brought the dog home just to show Jayme (a friend who was in the market for a dog), but he and Ralph are getting along SO WELL, you should see them. And, oh, I just love this little guy. He's really my heart dog. The boys think he's great. Would you even consider. . . ?"

Silence on my end.

"How important is this to you?" I finally asked. Terry and I have a 0-10 rating scale that we use to make all kinds of decisions. If we're haggling over an issue, but it's only a 2 for her and it's an 8 for me, it usually goes my way.

It took me a while to get her ranking on the dog, but finally she said he was a 9.

I smelled defeat.

I don't like playing the part of the big, bad, dog-hating mama. I just didn't want to end up in the same boat we used to be in when we had Paco. In the 16 years he lived with us, I never really bonded with him. Nevertheless, guess who made sure he was fed, trimmed his shaggy coat, even picked him up and carried him down the stairs when he was old and arthritic?

The rest of the family didn't seem that attached to him. Or so I thought.

Before we finally put Paco to sleep last March, our then-4-year-old talked about it for days. Our older son got weepy. The day the vet came to our house (bless her) to give him his injection, Terry and the boys were in tears. "Goodbye, Paco." Sniff, sniff. "You're the best dog."

We buried him in the back yard. We included a note to the angels, so they'd be sure to give him his favorite treats. We even included a box of biscuits. Then we covered him with dirt, put azalea blossoms on the ground, held hands and slowly circled the spot.

Even though I had said I'd never get a dog again ("When Paco goes, that's it!" I'd told everybody in my firmest voice), something in my heart opened up when I saw Noah patting the fresh dirt on Paco's grave.

I remembered his puckered face a few short weeks later when a woman at work found an abandoned dog at a convenience store. Kids really should have a pet, I said to myself with a sigh. If we get one now, Noah will be able to grow up with him. I agreed to meet the dog.

Soon, the newly dubbed Ralph was sleeping in David's room, and we were back into the routine of daily walks and feeding.

But a second dog? Give me a break.

Then Terry uttered the number "9" and my heart did that old expansion trick again.

I held my ground for exactly two hours. Mac (that's the new dog's name) has the second-cutest face I've ever seen. He, too, has short hair. At one point, the dogs looked at me and did that little tilt-of-the-head trick at the same time, looking adorable. (Terry, I'm sure, put them up to it.)

Within weeks, however, the honeymoon was over and I was prying Ralph's teeth off Mac's neck. (How did I get into this?) Friends say they're just trying to establish which one is the alpha dog.

"Hey," I've said to the two canines in my most authoritative voice, "I'm the top dog around here, not either of you."

But like everybody else in the household, they refuse to listen.

Jan. 9, 2001

A God-filled moment can illuminate our lives

It has taken me years to say the G-word out loud. You know, the one that ends in "D" and has an "O" in the middle.

Perhaps the reason is that I rejected the idea of a Supreme Being when I was 17, and my skin would crawl when people — especially family members — would say "God led them to this" and "God led them to that," and everything would be hunky-dory if I'd just turn my life over to God.

Of course, now that I'm a middle-aged believer, I'm more tolerant of God language. The word even occasionally slips from my own mouth.

Still, I'm particularly moved by people who manage to describe what I might call a God-filled moment without attributing it to you-know-who.

I'd like to share two such stories I've heard in the past year.

The first occurred during the movie "American Beauty." It's about two dysfunctional families that are neighbors. One dad wants to have sex with a teenage girl; the other father is homophobic and racist. One mom is a snob; the other is mentally ill. The teen-age boy, in particular, is creepy. He carries around a video camera and films people doing all kinds of things, any time of day.

About three-quarters of the way through the movie, the boy asks the girl next door whether she wants to see "the most beautiful thing I've ever filmed."

OK, here's the sappy part, I thought. We'll see a toddler in the park, or maybe puppies playing with a ball.

Hardly. On the screen is a brick wall with a few scattered leaves on the ground. But the focus is something else: a white plastic garbage bag being tossed by the wind.

"It was one of those days," the teen said, "when it's a minute away from snowing, and there's this electricity in the air, you could almost hear it. And this bag was — just — dancing — with me, like a little kid begging me to play with it — for *15 minutes.*

"That was the day I realized there was this entire life behind things and this incredibly benevolent force who wanted me to know that there was no reason for me to be afraid — ever.

"It's a poor excuse, I know, but it helps me remember. I need to remember."

The other story I heard one night at my book club. In the more than 10 years of the club's existence, we've covered almost every topic under the sun, but to my rec-ollection the G-word has never been mentioned.

While discussing a book by an American Indian author, one of the women suddenly started talking about a time when, alone in her room, feeling she had hit rock bottom, she asked for help.

"I couldn't help myself at that point," she said. "But as soon as I asked, I got it."

For a moment the room got quiet. Then we went on to other things. Several days later, I called to ask her to elaborate.

She was 45 years old at the time, she said, and an alco-holic. She had tried to stop drinking many times. After a week or so, she'd give herself a pat on the back — and then immediately go to the store and buy beer.

Six months earlier she had visited her father — also an alcoholic. Empty whiskey bottles lay all over his house. He'd sunk to an all-time low.

She was sinking, too. The drinking was starting to affect her work. One night, out of desperation, she got down on her knees.

"I can't do this myself," she said. "I need help."

Simple. Short. But the response was immediate. Right then and there, her desire to drink went away. In its place was a calmness and something she termed "friendliness."

She hasn't had a drink since.

She doesn't exactly know what helped her. (For years she just called it The Force.) And the experience didn't prompt her to go to church or pray in the conventional sense.

But occasionally, when the mood hits her, she stops what she's doing and whispers one word: "Thanks."

Feb. 6, 2001

Family life recedes when fever intrudes

For a week, my Mama Bear instincts disappeared.

I didn't care whether my boys ate cereal for dinner, drew blood during a fight, chucked their homework down the garbage disposal or sold the dogs to the highest bidder.

I was sick.

All I wanted to do was curl up in a ball in a perfectly quiet room with the shades pulled down. Other people's needs? Let them eat cake, I said. I'm going to pull this blanket over my head.

For at least five minutes, anyway.

Then there are kids to wake up, lunches to make, dishes to wash, phones to answer, laundry to put away, dogs to walk. These things don't stop for something as insignificant as a 103-degree temperature.

Of course, it could be worse. Terry could be sick. At least in between my tiny bursts of energy, I could lie down or sip tea while she kept the family going.

Three years ago, we weren't so lucky. All four of us were sick at the same time. Terry and I would look at each other and practically growl, "It's your turn to deal with the kids!" "I've got a fever!" "Well, mine is higher than yours!"

Even now I shudder when I think about that week. Noah was only 2 and could have killed himself while we lay comatose on the bed.

I felt nothing for my kids at the time. Nothing. It wasn't until the fever subsided and I could eat again that my love for them came rushing back.

How do chronically ill parents do it? Or single moms? Or parents in countries where illness is rampant and food is scarce?

I read once how a boy in a concentration camp watched his father die. Without even a tear in his eye, he tore into his father's pocket and gobbled down the bit of bread his father had hidden there.

OK, that may be a little too morbid. But thoughts like these get stirred up when you wake in the night with a pounding head, a shivering body and pain shooting up and down your back. When Terry mentioned last week that she might be getting sick, too, I thought, "Don't you dare!" All I could think was: Who's going to drive the kids to school? Who'll take the dogs out? Who'll make the matzo ball soup? Not I.

Now that I'm out of the woods, my Monster Self has receded. I can even appreciate the lessons learned: how ill people need all the help that healthy people can dish out, how we need each other to keep love alive during feverish nights and times of pain so intense that all else is blotted out.

If nothing else, we need silence, a dark room, a comfortable bed — and not a task in sight.

March 6, 2001

An 11-year-old's courage is contagious

The 11-year-old boy stood before the audience. The speech he was about to give was gutsy. His mother, squirming in her seat, wondered whether he'd gone too far.

"What does the word 'gay' mean to you?" the boy began. "Being gay means two men or two women who love each other. I, for one, do not understand what's so bad about this. Even though I'm not gay, my parents are, and I feel very strongly about this issue. . . .

"I have two moms instead of a mom and a dad, but everything else about my life is basically the same. We live in a normal house, in a normal neighborhood, and do pretty much normal stuff, like go on family trips, visit relatives and just have a good time. Of course, I also have to go to bed at a regular time, do chores and get in trouble sometimes, even if it's my little brother's fault. Is this that much different from your family?

"I find it very offending when people use 'gay' as a put-down or call something they dislike 'gay.' Even some of my friends use 'gay' as an insult. It hurts.

"According to a Des Moines, Iowa, public school survey, the average high school student hears anti-gay comments 26 times a day. Imagine how that would affect someone who is gay or who has gay family members or friends."

The applause after his speech was polite. Only when the principal announced that her son had won first place did the surprise come: The students jumped to their feet, clapping wildly.

The mother was stunned. At best, she thought the students would refrain from saying mean things. That they would actually *support* her son seemed unthinkable.

It wasn't that she'd been completely in the closet. Over the years, she and her partner had come out to teachers, neighbors, doctors, camp counselors. But those conversations always had been one-on-one, quiet, discreet. When her niece had told her son he didn't have a "family," the mother hadn't corrected her. She let people she just met assume she was married. At work, she let people know slowly, over time, never wanting to make it a big deal. At a previous job, when the boss had found out, he'd wanted to move her to a position where she wouldn't deal with the public. Although he'd never followed through, just knowing he'd even considered it made her more secretive.

She felt she moved in and out of safe environments as she would move in and out of air-conditioned buildings. Being gay was OK here, not OK there. This person was open, that person not. She grew accustomed to making quick judgment calls.

At bottom, the woman was afraid. For herself. For her partner. For her sons. They might be rejected, ridiculed. The thought that her son might suffer broke her heart.

And yet here he stood, broadcasting her story to the world. When the applause died down, her fear was replaced with pride. He took a stand. Spoke his mind. And, in a small way, changed the world.

As tears came to her eyes, she knew she would have to change, too. She needed to be who she was, in as many situations as possible.

Now a year has passed. Over that year she has come out of the closet a little more. She has referred to her partner to strangers, even using the word "she." But she never blatantly came out to the public. Until now.

I am that woman.

I am that gay person.

I am that lesbian mom.

April 17, 2001

It's a family tradition with wheels

My son Noah reaches out and grabs my hand. We're at a roller rink for his sixth-birthday party, skating around and around, hot air whizzing past our faces, "Ride With Me" by Nelly blaring over the speakers.

I'm in heaven. I love gliding over the floor to the rhythm of the song, smelling sweat and old skates, seeing the lights dim during "Couples Only," giggling during the hokeypokey.

For me, skating is a legacy. In a family splintered by distance and lifestyle, it's one of the few activities that span three generations. We don't own family land. We don't share family recipes. We don't even celebrate the same religious holidays.

But we have the experience of skating, a thin thread that winds through the years, loosely binding our disparate lives.

My parents met at a Chicago roller rink in 1949. They were 15 years old. My shy father eyed my mother from afar, noticing the skinny girl with long dark hair wearing a white blouse and dark skirt. Finally, he asked her to skate. She accepted.

But later, when he offered to drive her home, she refused. It wasn't until a week later that she agreed to let him — as long as her friend Darlene could go, too.

It was winter and the roads were icy. While my mom and Darlene jabbered away, my father struggled to keep control of the car. Would he get in an accident? Would he get her home on time? The car literally slid down the streets. He could see other cars that were already turned sideways. When he finally dropped her at her doorstep, he breathed a sigh of relief.

He told me this story the first time several years ago, when I was taping an interview with him for a family history project. My parents are not prone to telling stories — especially about themselves. I was glad I pried this one of him.

During their next several years of dating, my parents went skating every week. After they married and my two sisters and I were born, my mom would take us skating often.

I loved it from the start. My mother told me to stay around the edge so I could grab onto the side bars if I started to fall. But even at 4, I mastered the skates quickly and was soon inching out to the center black line with the big kids and grown-ups. It was one of the few times I disobeyed my mother.

The rink continued to be a familiar thread throughout my youth. We wouldn't go every week, but every so often we'd end up back there, circling the floor. It was the first place my parents would let me go alone with a friend. My seventh-grade class at St. Domitilla held a skating party there. When we moved to Fort Lauderdale when I was 13, the skating rink was one of the first places we went. There were differences — the floor was terrazzo instead of wood, they played records instead of the organ music we were used to — but the sense of flying was the same.

After I moved away as an adult, we would occasionally go skating when we got together to visit. My parents would take out their old skates with the wooden wheels and venture out to the floor. During Couples Only they'd cross arms and skate side by side, their legs moving in unison. Skating behind them, I'd see them lean into one another in a rare display of affection.

I fought back tears the day my father told me he'd never skate again. The last time he'd been at a rink, his inner ear caused him problems and he couldn't balance well. He didn't want to risk falling down. Just like that, his skating days were over.

So now I try to pass on the tradition to my children. Recently, I bought my first pair of Rollerblades and wore them to Noah's birthday party. After a few wobbly times around the rink, I caught the knack of the single blade of tiny wheels instead of the four large wheels.

After Noah grabbed my hand, my older son grabbed the other. Soon my spouse, Terry, caught up with us. For a few brief moments, there we were, skating four strong, the wind in our faces, the earth rushing beneath our feet.

June 5, 2001

A spiritual life comes in many guises

She called me condescending and judgmental.

I dismissed the accusations with a wave of the hand. I was just right, that's all.

I was arguing that people who said they weren't religious, but were instead spiritual, were copping out. Unless they were involved in some kind of spiritual practice — and, more important, involved with a spiritual community — they couldn't be going very deep.

Everybody's different, insisted Terry, my partner in life and love. Just because people don't pray and meditate all the time, or belong to an organized religious group, doesn't mean they can't spiritually evolve.

Does, too.

Does not.

This, ahem, *discussion* continued the next day. While riding my bike in the morning, I came up with what I thought was my best argument. When people say they're athletes, you assume certain things: They're involved with some kind of physical activity, they practice regularly, they at least occasionally hook up with like-minded people. They might be accomplished or mediocre, but they're committed.

I questioned whether people who say they're spiritual can make the same claim. They might feel connected to the universe while on the beach or hearing a piece of music, they might light a candle here or there, but there is no real substance. They aren't being *challenged*.

When I got home, I told Terry my analogy as she was walking out the door. She didn't buy it. I was being arrogant, she said. Just because I prayed a lot didn't mean I was better than she was. She, like a lot of people, didn't need the dependency on structured prayer or weekly religious services. She left in a huff.

Two hours later, the phone rang.

"Someone could be really interested in sports, watch it all the time, think it's great, but not be a player," she said after I'd barely gotten out a "hello." "They'd still be a sports enthusiast."

"But an enthusiast is not an athlete," I countered. Didn't she get it? Fifteen minutes later, we still hadn't made any headway.

Later that evening, still debating her in my head, I went into my bedroom to read. This was the night of the big storm and the six tornados. But even the crashing thunder didn't faze me much. Soon I was nodding off.

When a friend who was freaked out by the storm called after 10 p.m., Terry immediately told her to come over. Groggily, I got up and walked downstairs. This friend is like family, but still I felt my heart sinking. I hate when my sleep gets interrupted.

Then near midnight, we found out a nearby couple's house was flooded. Before I knew what was happening, Terry was down the street helping them and offering to have them stay at our house for the night.

When she told me this over the cellphone, I just sighed. Our house was a mess. I'd be embarrassed to have anyone stay over. I was relieved when she returned home alone and said they'd be staying someplace else.

As my head finally hit the pillow, I suddenly had a mental lightning flash. What good did all my praying do if, when people really needed help, I was more interested in crawling into bed rather than reaching out to offer support and comfort?

Terry hadn't thought twice about helping out. She never does. It's one reason I love her so much.

In the morning, even though the words stuck in my throat, I sheepishly said, "You were right."

She looked at me puzzled, but pleased.

During my prayers later that morning, I told God: "You knew what you were doing when you sent me this woman."

June 19, 2001

Life changes when son is at camp

"He'll be gone how long?" my friends asked.

"A month," I replied, watching their eyes widen in surprise.

It did sound like a long time, especially because David had never been gone for longer than a week. But he was 12 and dying to go to sleep-away camp.

Would I survive? Would he? Would *Terry*? In the two weeks before he left, she'd get emotional whenever she'd think about it. She had numerous conversations with the counselors beforehand: about fees (not cheap), David's diet (he's lactose-intolerant) and his unusual family situation (two moms). Luckily, this was a Jewish camp, and they were used to Jewish mothers. "Oh, no, you're not the only one who's been calling us," they reassured her.

The day we dropped David off, we were barely on the highway before Terry started crying. Only our 6-year-old, Noah, sitting in the back seat, could cheer her up. "Ima (that's *Mom* in Hebrew), I'll buy you a piece of candy with my own money, OK?"

Me, I sat in the seat beside her dry-eyed. I love David immensely — he's interested in everything, bubbles over with enthusiasm and has an adventurous spirit. But even in the five minutes since we'd dropped him off, I could feel the effects of going from two children to one.

Noah was quiet. No bickering. No one to punch. The nine-hour drive home was a breeze.

I don't know about your household, but in mine, everyone is a chief. I'm talking powerful personalities: opinionated, outspoken, don't-take-no-for-an-answer types. Before Noah was born, I worried that this strong-willed family would overwhelm him.

What a joke. He came barreling into the world feisty enough to take on all three of us. Needless to say, when we're all together, it can get rather rowdy and chaotic. (Just ask our neighbors.)

So when even one of us is gone, it's a relief, a respite, a chance to catch my parental breath.

There are other perks, too. Noah got both of his parents' undivided attention. He scarfed it up like a dry-food cat that suddenly gets a dish of tuna. I hardly had to discipline him all month.

And the house stayed neat. Once I cleaned David's room (which took me three days), it stayed that way. There were fewer crumbs on the counters, Band-Aid wrappers on the bathroom floor and shoes in the hallway.

When Noah went to sleep at night, the house was actually quiet. No radio playing, no kitchen cabinets opening and closing, no 11 p.m. experiments.

Feeling slightly guilty about enjoying David's temporary absence, I asked my sister — who has a 15-year-old away for six weeks this summer — how she was faring. Now, this is a supermom who home-schools her kids and watches over their every move. I assumed she'd be in deep grief.

"Well," she said, "it's been nice. It's certainly a lot quieter."

I chuckled into the phone receiver.

Of course, by the end of the four weeks, I was in need of a David fix. I wanted to see his sparkling face again, hear his laughter, watch him prance around with his earphones on and his radio clipped to his pants pocket.

When we met up with him at his grandparents' house in North Carolina, he had grown taller and more confident. He had adventures to tell. He gave us presents and even wrapped Noah in a bear hug.

But it didn't take long for normal life to resume. Within five minutes of walking through the front door, Noah knocked a sign off David's door. David punched Noah. I yelled.

Break time was over.

July 31, 2001

We avert our eyes from sweatshop misery

After my 12-year-old son cleans both bathrooms, I ask him to take the dishes out of the dishwasher. "That, too?" he groans, slumping his shoulders and heaving a big sigh.

When it's time for my 6-year-old to take vegetable scraps out to the compost bin, he has a meltdown. It stinks! It's gross! No way! When a friend stops by, he tells her, "Mom is *torturing* me!"

I recall these reactions when I see the cover of *Co-op America Quarterly* at New Leaf Market. Underneath the face of a solemn child it reads: "Guide to Ending Sweatshops."

My vision blurs, and for a moment the child on the cover is Noah. I blink, and the face changes to David. I look away, a knot forming in my chest.

I know that many of the people in these sweatshops are children. Young children. Like Alamgir Rasid from Bangladesh, who worked in a garment factory when he was a little older than Noah. From 7:30 a.m. to 10:30 p.m. he cut threads in the finishing section, over and over and over.

In Punjab, Tahira Bibi stitched soccer balls together at his home for 32 cents a ball. His fingers swelled, but no matter. He kept to the task. He was a year younger than David.

When he was 5, Shravan Kumar was kidnapped and forced to work at a carpet loom for 19 hours a day. My mind can't even compute this. A 5-year-old? This torture was real.

You've probably heard similar stories. Just last month, we ran a Knight Ridder series about slave labor in West Africa. The challenge is how to keep these stories alive, in our conscious minds, and not let them be tucked away in a file that's labeled "Don't go there."

That's what I tend to do. Trying to face that pain is like trying to walk into a flame. I get close to the heat and quickly veer away. I distract myself. I shake it off. Even if verbally I'm still clucking about how horrible it is, in my heart I'm already distancing myself. I go back to my life where children have soft, tender hands and their cries in the night are answered.

This time, however, I force myself to take one small step. I buy the magazine. I read it. I vow to write those letters, boycott certain products, pass the word on.

But when I think about it too much, I see the eyes of children halfway around the world reflected in my children's eyes. It's enough to double me over. After breaking down in tears the other day (in front of my child, no less, who didn't know what was wrong), I allowed myself to be distracted again. The flame could wait until another day.

But I don't want to go numb. I'm going to take a cue from my colleague, Karen Olson, who encounters suffering people all the time when reporting for her column, the Caring Connection. Next to her computer, she keeps a picture of a starving mother and child with the words of Mahatma Gandhi underneath: "Recall the face of the poorest and most helpless person you have seen and ask yourself if the next step you contemplate is going to be of any use to that person."

I tear off the cover of *Co-op America*. I tape it up on the wall next to my computer, right beside a picture of my sons. I stare at David's and Noah's eyes. I stare at the girl's eyes. They are the same.

Aug. 14, 2001

Electronic beasts
can rule a home

Ever watch meat-eaters react to a vegetarian? Backs arch slightly. Voice tones change. They insist they love their red meat, or they make a sneering reference to tofu ("I ate it once and almost threw up!"), or they laughingly repeat the bumper-sticker message: "I didn't climb my way up the food chain to eat vegetables."

I think it's because, deep down, we know that we shouldn't be chomping on the flesh of a formerly live creature. But we don't want to give it up, so we make excuses.

I think TV and computer games produce a similar reaction in parents. In our better moments we know most of this stuff is junk, but kids love it, or we want a break (this is my most-often-used reason), or everyone in the whole damn culture seems to be using them, so we acquiesce.

That's why I'm so grateful for periodically running into people who severely limit — or, better yet, banish — these electronic beasts. Without their example, I'd be feeding the monsters my family's prime time.

My oldest son was still an infant when I ran into my first limited-TV couple. They had two children who were 4 and 6. While I was visiting one day, the kids were just finishing up their TV time — one hour a day of public television.

You could actually set limits like this? As a new parent, I was impressed. I vowed to try the same thing with my kid.

And I did. I added a few variations — the Discovery Channel was OK with me, too — but for the most part I toed the line.

Then I had a second child.

By the time this one was running around — and I mean running — I found myself in desperate need of a break by late afternoon. That's when our TV watching expanded.

Suddenly, more channels were added to the mix. The hour crept into an hour and a half. The older one didn't want to watch what the younger one did, so the TV was on longer. I felt like a cop, trying to time when one show finished and the other went on. Invariably, Terry or I'd get talking on the phone or doing a chore and, oops, they'd been on for two hours.

Then one day my editor mentioned that she didn't allow her children — now in their late teens and early 20s — to watch any TV on school nights. I'd heard this idea before, but I'd never known anybody in the flesh who'd done it. If she could do it, so could I.

Surprisingly, my kids didn't squawk much when we laid down the new rule. Within days, we were in our new routine and my cop duties were over. Sometimes I'm tempted to relent (again, when I want that break), but I think of my editor and resist.

Then there are computer games.

We've always tried to enforce the No Target rule — anything that had to be hunted down and blasted was not allowed. Since this accounts for 95 percent (my estimate) of the games out there, my sons are rarely on the computer.

But one day a Game Boy sneaked into the house. It was a hand-me-down from a friend. Although I have a particular loathing for these things, I let it go for a while.

At least we hadn't had to spend a lot of money on it, I rationalized.

But within three weeks, Terry and I were pulling our hair out. We couldn't get our sons' attention. Trying to put a time limit on it just added to our cop duties. We felt out of control.

Then I discovered one boy whose parents limited "screens" and another whose parents banned them altogether. One of the kids had just driven hundreds of miles from New England to Tallahassee. What did he do in the car? He read. He sketched (he always kept a sketch book with him). He looked out the window and daydreamed.

Emboldened by their example, we banned Game Boy from the house. Even friends who come over can't turn one on. I'd like to say we didn't hear any squawks about this one, but we did. Loud ones.

But we've never regretted making the decisions. When the kids grow up, they might have to seek therapy because of their "screenless" childhood. ("My mother actually *threw* the Game Boy in the trash!")

But I think it's worth it.

Now if I could just stop eating chicken. . . .

Sept. 4, 2001

Terrible events leave parents numb, kids confused

The night after two airplanes crashed into the World Trade Center, my 12-year-old son and I were glued to the TV set. Every once in a while I'd glance over at him and ask, "Are you OK?"

After his quick nod, we'd zero back in on the tube. I know I should have talked to him more, helped him sort through his feelings, given him a chance to vent or ask questions.

But I couldn't.

Instead, he ended up coming over to me, putting his arm around my shoulder and saying, "Are *you* all right? I think you're taking this harder than me."

In the numbing aftermath of Tuesday's events, I had a hard time keeping my parental hat on. Terry and I managed to make two quick decisions. First, we didn't allow our 6-year-old son to watch any of the events on TV. We felt he was too young, and we didn't want images of people jumping out of buildings and towers bursting into flames to give him nightmares.

Of course, he picked up on the charged atmosphere anyway. Sitting at the dinner table in tears, he wailed, "This is the biggest story of my life and you're not letting me watch!" Later, when he caught a glimpse of the falling towers from the bathroom door after his bath, he shrugged, "It's just two towers falling down. What's the big deal?" Needless to say, we didn't point out the number of people crumpled beneath the rubble.

David, on the other hand, was old enough to know what was going on. He's a current-events junkie who listens to National Public Radio practically nonstop. We suspended our no-TV-on-school-nights rule to let him watch the TV reports.

With those parameters set, Terry and I didn't focus much on the boys. We were occupied with our own ricocheting feelings of numbness, outrage, sorrow and fear.

It was 10 p.m. before I came out of my fog and realized that David had watched TV for five straight hours.

"You need to go to bed," I said.

Suddenly, the kid who had claimed all day that he was OK couldn't go to sleep. I sat down near his bed and rubbed his back.

"Mom, they showed Palestinian kids waving flags," he said, frowning. "They were *happy* about it."

Normally, I'd launch into my rap about not assuming all Palestinians feel that way, that's just one quick news clip, be careful not to stereotype. Being a Jewish family, we've had this discussion many times.

But the image of rejoicing Palestinians made me sick to my stomach. Even though I knew there were historical reasons for their response, at the moment I couldn't have cared less. With a lump in my throat, I decided the big-picture lecture would have to wait for another day.

Today, a week after the terrorist attacks, I've yet to have a serious discussion with my kids about what happened. Terry, who's a therapist and has processed numerous tragedies with clients, isn't much better at talking to the kids than I am.

"I just can't," she said, her eyes looking away.

Although she had one brief conversation with David over the weekend, for the most part we watched the latest reports. We read the paper. We hugged our kids tightly.

It will take rescue workers months to clean up the debris in New York and Washington, to sift through the wreckage for clues, signs of life, to find a final resting place for all the scattered fragments. So it will be with our emotional lives. We'll search, sift, perhaps find meaning, one piece at a time.

Sept.18, 2001

Driven to distraction by furry, furtive invaders in the wall

While the United States has been scrambling to rout out terrorists worldwide, I've been fighting gangster-types on my own home turf. These criminals are noisy and bold one moment, sneaky the next. You never know when or where they'll show up. First they come for a visit; then they take over. Your life means nothing.

You might call them squirrels. I, however, am joining those who spit out a more technical term: *rodents*. After being kept awake numerous nights, I no longer think those bushy tails are so cute.

We started our war against the gnawers last year. First we just heard a scratching sound inside our bedroom wall. Then there was mad scampering to and fro. Before we knew it, a whole troop had moved in.

Animal-loving, nonviolent people that we are, we didn't want to harm the little darlings. We would never (gasp!) *poison* them. We called one of those pest-control places that promised not to use nasty chemicals.

Instead, the guy put up a small screen door over the hole. That way, he told us, the squirrels could get out but not back in.

Didn't work.

Then he left the screen door open, hoping the open hole would lure the furry creatures out.

Never happened.

Finally, he cut two 4-by-4-inch holes high in our bedroom wall — to see whether he could capture them coming out that way and bring them outside. Not even a sign of a twitching nose.

In desperation, he left us his ladder (tall enough for our two-story house) and staple gun. We spent hours opening the screen door during the day and waiting for them to come out so we could slam it shut and staple it securely. It took us days.

Finally, we could get a full night's sleep.

Then this fall, they came back. We frantically searched the eaves for a hole they could get into, but we didn't find one. A couple of friends helped us try the screen-door routine again.

No luck.

Just as I was thinking that assassination sounded pretty good, we came up with one final plan: Put mothballs near the screen door and in the holes we'd made in the bedroom wall last year. (We had put the Sheetrock back in place but never patched them up.) We used a whole box of mothballs.

Within an hour, our house reeked so much that David was gagging and Terry could barely breathe. Even outside, the smell billowed out in invisible clouds, coating our hair and clothes.

"I can't live like this!" Terry wailed.

Luckily, we did see one fat squirrel scramble out of a hole in the back of the house, giving away the secret entrance. We figured no living creature could exist in the walls with that smell, so we removed the mothballs and put a new screen over the back hole.

Later that night, I heard my first scratching noise. I wanted to scream. I wanted revenge. Those squirrels were dead meat.

Next morning, when I took out my garbage, I saw a squirrel frantically chewing away the wood around the screen door, desperate to get inside. She didn't run away when I approached. She glared at me with hard, dark eyes. I glared back. It was a standoff.

Then suddenly, I realized: There were babies inside that screen door. This wasn't a terrorist. This was just a mama, trying to make a good life for her young 'uns. I could relate to that.

That afternoon, I opened the screen door one last time. I sat in my rocking chair on the lawn, waiting for the mama to come get her babies. After 45 minutes, I gave up. I climbed back up the ladder, closed the screen door and went inside. Within minutes, the mama was back, gnawing at the wood.

This time, I went back into the house after I opened the screen door. More than 20 feet below and from the other side of my house, my two sons and I watched from the window with binoculars.

"I think she's coming!" my 6-year-old yelled.

We held our breath. Come on, Mama, come and get 'em.

Finally, she came rushing down through the trees and onto the electric wire connected to our house. She looked around. Her tail twitched. Then she was inside the hole. A minute later she came out, a baby wrapped around her neck like a muffler.

Would she come back for a second one? Sure enough, a few minutes later she practically flew back down and shot through the hole. We cheered as she carried the second one away.

I think we have truly licked it this time. We haven't heard a noise in days.

But if they do come back, they should be forewarned: BB guns aren't that expensive.

Oct. 9, 2001

Pacifist ideals are tested by terrorism

"My father was killed two weeks after my fifteenth birthday. Some men walked into his office and shot him and my cousin, Luche, who was helping out as a receptionist. She was nineteen years old." (Juan Elias from Colombia)

Did the deaths prevent Juan from continuing his work in the children's peace movement?

At first, yes. He sat by their coffins, trying to make sense of it all. *"Why two in my family? Why my dad? Why my dad! And why Luche?"*

Suddenly, the civil war that had been going on all his life —all his parents' lives— took on new meaning. Yes, he had watched his middle-class lifestyle degenerate into poverty. Yes, his family had received death threats, his house had been bombarded with bullets, he'd seen blood in the streets. But nothing quite this close.

"I realized that no matter how much you want peace, you take a step towards violence when the war hits you personally."

Juan, who only six weeks earlier had met with young peace activists all over Colombia, got a gun. If anyone tried to kill him, he'd take a few people down with him. His family continued to get threats. Whenever they left the house, they were followed.

Life was now a blur. Nothing felt safe. The house felt strange. He missed his father.

One night, from a darkened kitchen window, he watched a man in the garden outside look up to the second story, where his relatives were visiting. The man was holding a gun.

Juan froze. Now was the time to get his own gun. No one would blame him. Heck, that's what people would expect: for him to protect his family.

But he didn't move. He thought of his work in the peace movement. He thought of his father's work. Two years earlier, the two of them had worked together to pass a referendum to convert their town into a model for peace. Killing this man would not help him, his family or his country. *"How can I become violent now?"* he asked himself.

He stood still.

Eventually, the man turned and walked away. Not long afterward, Juan got rid of his gun.

I read this story in "Out of War: True Stories from the Front Lines of the Children's Movement for Peace in Colombia," by Sara Cameron. The story hit home. Since Sept. 11, my pacifist ideals have gone underground. I don't know where I stand anymore. As the deaths of Juan's father and cousin felt to him, the terrorism on American soil felt to me. Like Juan, I felt myself leaning toward violent solutions.

A few weeks ago I rented the movie "Gandhi" to remind myself of my old ideals. I watched it with my 12-year-old son so he could be exposed to the pacifist politics I now find difficult to espouse. When I heard Gandhi say that an eye for an eye would leave the whole world blind, I knew he was right. That's pretty much what's happening in Israel and the Occupied Territories right now. Nobody is *winning*. Everyone is sinking.

But it wasn't until I read Juan's story that I felt some of my old resolve coming back. *How can I become violent now?* What would it mean to work for peace during a time like this? Is there a way to wage peace at the same time that we wage war?

I don't have any answers. I'm still confused.

But Juan's example helps. He had to dig pretty deep inside himself to get rid of that gun. Perhaps I could dig a little deeper, too.

Oct. 30, 2001

Silence reveals gunk, pearls

"A week?" squeaked my incredulous hairdresser. "You're going to be silent for a week?"

She made it sound like a jail sentence. But it seemed like heaven to me.

As a reporter who is constantly in yak mode and as the mother of two boys — *noisy* boys who require endless warnings, cajolings, nighttime stories and answers to "Mom!" "Mom!" "Mom!" — I figured that not speaking for an entire week at Elat Chayyim, a Jewish retreat center in New York, would be spiritual balm.

Of course, until you get there, you don't realize how LOUD silence can be. Stop speaking, stop listening to TV, radio, spouse and kids, stop distracting yourself every other second — and suddenly the stirrings of your own mind and soul pick up volume.

What you hear isn't always pleasant. I, for one, heard a lot of gunk.

But right alongside all that garbage, I got a few pearls — sublime messages that filled my soul and have been feeding me ever since.

First, the gunk.

At Elat Chayyim we weren't supposed to just be silent. We were supposed to meditate. We were to focus on our breath — for numerous half-hour sessions. If your mind started to wander, you were to bring your attention back to your breath.

That's it.

I thought I would jump out of my skin. My mind wouldn't settle down. I'd take one breath with attention and then start to wander. Take another attentive breath, then wander again. Sometimes I'd want to shout at the timekeeper, "Ring that bell! I can't do this anymore!"

Part of the reason for meditating is to observe the mind, to see how we're rarely in the present moment. Instead, we're always thinking about what we'll do next, or what happened yesterday, or last week, or 10 years ago. We are always someplace else but here — *anyplace* else but here.

When you're in the present moment, you settle down. You're attentive. You're at peace. You're filled with compassion.

Our teachers reassured us that this could take years of practice. We weren't to despair. Just keep on meditating.

So I kept on. But I was disgusted with what I was finding inside my mind. Envy, for one thing. Whenever someone would answer a teacher's question (the one time we could talk during the week), I turned green. I wanted to be the smart one. I wanted the attention.

And then there was the judgmental side of me. Even though I didn't talk to anyone the entire week, I was sizing up everyone. This one was a showoff. That one was cocky. This one was better than I. That one was worse.

But right when I thought I'd give up this meditating — it wasn't doing much for my self-esteem — I'd have one of those sublime moments. I'll tell you about two.

I can't tell you exactly which moment the first one happened. But what I learned is burned into my memory.

It came in a flash, as if I'd walked into a darkened room and turned on the light for a split second. I didn't have time to look around much, get the contents of the room in detail. But I saw enough. It was love.

I realized, for the first time and on a bone level, that love was part of the DNA of the universe. Sounds schmaltzy, a "love is all around" thing. But I realized it was true.

Just the way you take a sample of your hair, lung, eye or toenail and find those 23 pairs of chromosomes, so it was with love. From the outside it might be hard to discern. But look deep enough, put it under a powerful enough microscope, and there they'd be, those love chromosomes, waving back at you.

This gave me tremendous comfort — and courage. Comfort to know that love was available to everyone, at all times. Courage because it could never run out. It would always be there to help me.

The other moment came near the end of the retreat. After days of silence, a teacher suggested we find a place by ourselves to talk out loud to God. The only trick was to keep on talking, no matter what, for a specific time. If you stopped to think, to find the right words, you were analyzing too much. You were supposed to just speak from the heart.

When I did, God spoke two words back: Grow up.

I heard them almost as if they were audible. Man, I thought, God sure doesn't mince words. At first they seemed harsh, but after a while I found them to be full of wisdom and kindness. I did need to grow up.

From the outside, I'm sure, I seemed like a responsible adult — I was a good parent, I did my work, I paid my taxes. But inside I was a whiner. "This isn't right." "I don't like that." "How come I have to do this?" "This is too hard." Poor, poor, pitiful me.

I promised God that day that I would try to grow up. And I have grown up, at least a little. When situations arise that I don't like, I ask myself, "How would a grown-up handle this?" It's amazing how it stops the whining.

So in the end, I'd say the gunk was worth it. Silence may be a stern taskmaster, but ultimately it leads right back to the love chromosomes.

Jan. 19, 2002

Spend time with the children of gays

The American Academy of Pediatrics recently announced support for gays adopting because, basically, gay parents are no different from heterosexual ones.

I have two words in response: Well, duh.

I don't mean to be dismissive. It's just that those of us who have been raising our children here on the ground level know this already. We've seen it in action. A new pronouncement by some "credible" organization stating the obvious seems almost silly: "Studies show that loving parents are good for children!"

I guess unless you've seen it in flesh and blood, one could *theoretically* say it's not such a good idea. But I bet the hearts of even hardened conservatives would melt if they read in "An American Family" about Michael Galluccio's first encounter with the infant he and his partner, Jon, would later adopt. This 3-month-old was premature. He was HIV-positive. He had hepatitis C, tuberculosis, respiratory problems and a hole in his heart. He trembled from drug withdrawal.

When Michael and Jon walked into the group home where the infant was staying, they found him in a baby swing.

Michael wrote:

"The baby was staring right at me. For what seemed like hours, all I beheld was the sight of this child and the click-click, click-click of the baby swing. I stared at the baby and

in an instant I fell deeply in love for the second time in my life. There would be nothing I would not do for him. My son. He was sick, and he might be dying, and he was beautiful."

Sounds like a dad to me.

Instead of reading studies, those judges, legislators, adoption agencies or religious folk who question the wisdom of allowing gays to adopt should spend time around the children of gays and lesbians. As long as you're thinking in the abstract, you might want to debate gays adopting. But when it's in front of you, your worries may melt.

When I first told my mother over the phone that my partner, Terry, and I were expecting a baby, she gasped.

"Oh, my God. (Pause.) I'll talk to you later."

Click.

When I was pregnant with my second child, the response wasn't much better. Silence. My two sisters didn't speak to me until months after Noah was born.

It's not that my relatives are bigoted, unkind or unloving. They'd never had much exposure to gays; their religion didn't condone gay relationships; and they just didn't approve.

And they probably still don't. But they sure love our kids.

I treasure the image of my father playing cards with Noah, then about 4 years old, inside the camper trailer one night in Central Florida. They were playing War. (Terry, who didn't like that name, renamed it Struggle.) It was my father's turn to lay a card down. Noah's bright eyes looked up coaxingly, and he pointed his index finger at him as if to say "Your turn." They went on this way for hours.

Another time, after my parents had come to visit us and were about to return to South Florida, my older son, David, looked gloomy. He didn't want them to go. Even though he didn't say anything out loud, my mother picked up on it instantly and wrapped an arm around his shoulder. "We'll see you soon," she said reassuringly.

Then one day, without any prompting, Mom said, "I think you and Terry are doing a good job of raising the boys."

I almost fell over.

But that's the way of the human heart. Love goes right to the source.

Michael Galluccio writes about his father's first meeting with his and Jon's new son, Adam. Initially, his father was cool, smiling weakly from the back of the room. Then Michael's mother, who had been cooing over the baby, coaxed him over.

"Dad moved forward and took Adam from my mother. He held the baby up in front of him and looked him in the face. The man of fifty-seven and the child just three months old stared at each other, man to man, for a long, long moment. Dad gazed at Adam. Adam gazed gravely back. I watched as my father's eyes began to glisten and then thicken with tears. When he blinked, the tears ran down his face and he held Adam tightly to him."

Sounds like a granddad to me.

Feb. 19, 2002

Yours might be golf; mine is religion

My colleague Gerald Ensley wrote that he just doesn't "get" religion.

I had to laugh. We all have our irrational passions.

One of mine is religion. One of Gerald's is sports.

And I just don't get it.

In his March 31 column, he expressed dismay over priests who molested children, over an evangelist who made anti-Semitic remarks, over a man accused of plowing into the Tallahassee Islamic Center only to call himself a "religious person."

I don't understand the blind devotion to Bibles and Qurans written by men 2,000 years ago. I don't understand why there would be a heaven and a hell. I don't understand the centuries of violence and intolerance by those who believe their religious faith is better than another group's religious faith. It's all too illogical and magical for me.

And yet, he goes on to say, he knows folks — people he loves and respects — who do get a lot out of religion. Maybe it's not all bad. Near the end of the column, he admits, "Their faith will not diminish my life."

Couldn't the same be said for sports?

A boxer gets his ear bitten off. A dad kills another dad at their children's hockey game. One skater hires a hit man to whack another skater in the legs so she can win a competition. Athletes are arrested for domestic violence, rape, stealing and drunken driving.

It's all too illogical for me.

I don't understand the blind devotion to "Monday Night Football." I don't understand the thrill of doing things with balls — getting them past a line in the grass, plunking them down a hole, hitting them over a net. I don't understand the ferociousness of fans who actually get *depressed* when their team loses because they're convinced they're better than the other side. Some people even get stampeded to death in stadiums.

And yet . . . people I know and respect like sports. They talk about the challenge, the striving for perfection, the sheer enjoyment of watching a play in motion. I actually know somebody who trains for a triathlon so she can swim 2.4 miles, run 26.2 miles and bike 112 miles.

She says it's good for her. Who am I to argue?

Despite my initial reluctance, I signed up my 6-year-old for soccer. The first day he wore his purple uniform, he was beaming. When he made his first — and only — goal, he was so proud I thought he'd bust. When he got a medallion at the end of the season, he wore it for days.

Maybe this stuff isn't all bad.

My friend John Pekins wrote a book of poems about golf with his buddy Pete LeForge. Golf! You can write 29 poems about *golf*?

Find hole. Raise club. Whack! Is there (yawn) more to it than that?

John wrote: *sunlight / water / flowers / swoosh of wings / emerald turf / exhilaration / fear / all converge / where the club strikes ball*

and all hope / joy, / and gratitude / go flying / out toward the blue sky / rising / arcing / falling back / somewhere on the manicured turf / or in the trees / or out past the boundaries / bordering them . . .

then we pick up our bags / and walk to the next shot, /
sun in the sky, / water glistening below / alive with birds.

Other people's sports will not diminish my life. If I have the eyes to see, they actually might enhance it.

April 2, 2002

God's voice could calm Middle East

Every Rosh Hashanah, Jews read the Torah portion about Abraham's willingness to sacrifice his son Isaac. I've never been able to get much meaning from the story. I think if God had asked Sarah to kill her son, she would've flat out said "No!" Why was Abraham such a wimp?

Recently, I heard a rabbi provide a fresh angle to this puzzling piece of Scripture. More important, she provided insight into the Middle East today.

God says: "Abraham, I love you."

Abraham answers: "I love you, too, God."

God says: "I love you."

Abraham answers: "Yeah, God. I love you, too. I want to prove it to you."

God says: "Abraham, I love you."

Abraham is distracted now. He's thinking hard. "You deserve the very best, God. (Pause.) I know what I must do."

Other people sacrificed their children to the gods. He wouldn't be outdone. He would offer Isaac.

God tries to say something more. But Abraham isn't listening. He's on a mission. He packs up his donkey. He takes Isaac to the top of the hill. He ties Isaac to the altar.

Rumbling off in the distance is God's voice. It's getting louder, but Abraham is focused on his task. He's sweating. He raises the knife.

"Noooooooooooooo!!!!"

God's voice finally breaks through. "Abraham, Abraham! Do not lay your hand on the boy! This is not what I want!"

Abraham looks up. His mind clears. He can hear. He can see. The alternative is right there before him — the ram in the thicket.

He lets his child go.

I picture a Palestinian, a bomb strapped to his waist. He walks into the marketplace. An Israeli teenager saunters by. The man's finger moves toward the trigger.

An Israeli soldier sees a Palestinian home. He points his tank at the front door. The tank's treads start to move. A woman screams.

A Palestinian youth clutches a rock in his hand. His arm swings back.

An Israeli sniper sees movement inside a Palestinian building. He aims his gun.

Then softly, almost imperceptibly, the sky rumbles. The sound grows louder, then louder still. A fierce wind begins to blow. The Palestinian's hand stops inches from the trigger. The Israeli soldier slows his tank. The youth drops his arm. The soldier pulls back his gun.

With a clap of thunder, the sky suddenly breaks open. "Noooooooooo!!! This is not what I want! THIS IS NOT (pause) WHAT — I — WANT!"

The alternative is right there before them. Simple. Obvious. A two-state solution.

We must let the violence go.

May 27, 2002

Mothers know their value, and that's good enough

Enola Aird, director of the Motherhood Project, recently told a reporter: "America needs to recognize and appreciate the tremendous value mothers add to their children's lives and, therefore, to the whole society."

I hate to say it, honey, but it ain't gonna happen.

Moms — especially so-called stay-at-home moms — have been angling for respect for decades, to no avail. Occasionally, you'll hear gushy sentiments about how moms shape the minds of the next generation, and what could be more important than *that*?

But in reality, most people find mothers about as interesting as dirt — needed, perhaps, for growing things, but not somebody to seek out for interesting conversation at a cocktail party.

Frankly, I agree. Motherhood is boring, sometimes dreadfully so. The day-to-day drip, drip, drip of mothering is one big yawn. Nothing exciting about changing that fifth diaper of the day or folding that sixth load of laundry.

Sure, you might watch your toddler do something cute, have a meaningful conversation with your teenager, laugh uproariously with your 5-year-old.

But most of the time, you're doing grunt work.

Men know this. That's why they haven't been breaking down the doors to stay at home with the kids. While women have practically stampeded into the professional world in the last 30 years, only a trickle of men have chosen to be stay-at-home dads.

As a part-time worker, I inhabit that gray area between professional woman and at-home mom. Three days a week I dress up and march out the door to the office; four days I'm in jeans doing the school-volunteer, field-trip-chaperone, baby-on-my-hip thing.

And I can tell you, I get way more respect for my paid work than my unpaid work. But who cares?

Even with all the grunt work involved, mothering gives me more — and longer-lasting — job satisfaction.

Eventually, those drip, drip, drips add up to something. Sometimes it's very subtle. Your teenager decides to sweep the roof and clean the gutters without your even asking. Your 7-year-old puts one hand on his chest and the other hand on his dog, which will be put to sleep the following day. "You'll always be in my heart," he says, tears streaming down his face.

Responsibility and compassion don't spring out of nowhere. They're often the result of zillions of parenting moments that no one else knows about.

Mothers do their work for the same reason poets write poetry. Not for status, not for money, not because it's easy (anyone who has spent all day revising two lines of poetry knows this), but because we have some wild belief that nothing is more essential than this.

So let's stop whining about lack of respect. Others can be recognized and valued. We already know our worth.

Nov. 26, 2002

Let a child follow your spiritual lead

In interfaith or even interdenominational families, some parents say they want to expose their children to both religions. They don't want to push either one. The children, they reason, can make their own decisions.

I think that may be a mistake.

Let a child decide, and most likely you'll end up with confusion — or apathy. Religion isn't a spectator sport. We don't teach our children what it means to be a family by letting them observe how the neighbors do it. We "do" family right at home. To know what it's really all about, you have to see it — and feel it — from the inside.

Dozens of my friends might want my head on a platter for saying all of this, but I'm speaking partly from experience. When our first child was born, Terry and I were unclear about religion. She was Jewish. I was raised Catholic. Neither one of us was very observant.

"We'll be both!" we decided. What could be more open-minded? We celebrated Passover and Hanukkah. We occasionally attended services at a church that accepted our alternative family. I learned a few *berakot* (Jewish blessings); Terry managed to sing a few hymns.

And our son? By the time he was 4, he was puzzled. He'd ask, more than once, "I'm both Christian *and* Jewish, right, Mom?"

What was even worse, he didn't really know much about either religion. And neither did Terry or I. In our attempt to be open-minded, we ended up only shallow. We had yet to mature into religious adults.

Finally, we decided to just practice Judaism.

From the minute we made that decision, our religious experience deepened. We threw ourselves into the Jewish holidays. We started celebrating Shabbat dinners every Friday night. We enrolled our son in religious school. This year, after long and careful consideration, I converted.

My second son, who has been brought up completely Jewish, wrote down on this year's Thanksgiving list: "I'm thankful that my family and I are Jewish." My older son, now 13, wears a Star of David proudly and actually *enjoys* going to services. I'm confident that, when she's old enough, my infant daughter will express similar sentiments.

But even if she doesn't, she won't have a choice — at least until she's well into her teens.

In the meantime, in the name of open-mindedness, I try to expose my children to other religions. When my children visit my parents, I encourage them to go to Mass. When the local Islamic mosque has an open house, I take my older son. When my friends celebrated Buddha's birthday, my kids participated. I consider these wonderful opportunities to learn and grow.

But I want my children to experience them from a rooted place. Religion isn't some academic concept; it's a living reality.

I'm not suggesting that parents convert in the name of family unity. That may not be appropriate. But having children be "both" may mean that they really aren't either.

Helping our children find a spiritual home is part of our job as parents. Let's not leave them standing outside the door.

Dec. 10, 2002

Homosexuality is an easy scapegoat for churches

It's come up again — homosexuality and the church.

This time it's the National City Christ Church in Washington, D.C. Early this month, the board of elders agreed to perform same-sex marriages. Now some of the denominational leaders are outraged. Rescind your decision or be cut off from the Christian Church (Disciples of Christ), said the executive director of Disciple Renewal.

Ah. Homosexuality as litmus test. Hardly a week goes by that we don't hear about one church or another wrangling with this issue.

And I have to ask: Why?

Sure, the Bible makes a few negative references to homosexuals. But the Bible says a lot about a lot of things. Why is this issue getting stuck in everyone's craw?

Some might say it's our society's obsession with sex. Others claim it undermines heterosexual marriage.

But I have another theory: It's easy.

At best, gays make up only 10 percent of the population. Of those, few go to church — partly because churches haven't been all that welcoming. So it's not as if there are hordes of gays pounding on the church doors crying, "Let me in! Let me in!" Many don't want in, thank you very much.

This makes gays an easy target. What do churches have to lose by slamming people who are probably either in the closet or don't go to church at all?

If righteous religious folks really wanted to be brave, they'd tackle the issue of divorce. After all, Jesus never said anything about gays in the Gospels, but he did have a few choice words about divorce: *Everyone who divorces his wife and marries another commits adultery, and he who marries a woman divorced from her husband commits adultery.* (Luke: 16:18)

Of course, this issue affects a much larger proportion of congregants. Almost one in four Presbyterians is divorced. Almost 30 percent of Baptists are. Even the Catholic Church, one of the last bastions of the no-divorce rule, is slipping. In 1968, fewer than 600 annulments were granted in the United States. Today that number has jumped to more than 600,000. (Atheists, by the way, have the same divorce rate as Catholics: 21 percent.)

And then there's the clergy itself: The divorce rate is about the same as the general population's.

Granted, some churches are trying to stem the tide by offering premarital counseling or mentoring programs for those already married. But no one goes ballistic when a divorced person wants to remarry. Regardless of what Jesus said, many ministers go right on and perform the ceremony.

Spiritually speaking, I don't think it's important whether a person is gay or divorced. But if people are going to get on their high horse by taking the Bible literally, they should be consistent.

I challenge religious leaders to tackle the divorce issue first, before they even bring up the gay one. Be courageous. Take a stand. Create a new litmus test.

And leave your scapegoating days behind.

Dec. 24, 2002

Whole community must honor marriage commitment

A friend of mine who recently got married originally planned a very small wedding. She and her partner had already made vows to each other. He was shy, and getting up in front of a large group of folks made him nervous.

But in the end, at the urging of friends and family members, they invited a lot of people to the reception.

Excellent choice. We've all heard the saying that it takes a village to raise a child. Well, it also takes a village to sustain a marriage.

Marriage is a living organism that can be nourished by many roots, but one of the deepest is community. Without that root, the organism is likely to die.

Think of the long-term marriages you know — the vital ones in which the people respect each other, have fun together, laugh a lot — and most likely you'll see numerous tentacles that reach beyond their nucleus of two. They're connected to extended family. They participate in schools, religious congregations, neighborhoods, civic organizations, sports. They don't have to do the exact same thing, play the exact same role or be joined at the hip, but they're in there together. They share a vision.

A you-and-me-against-the-world attitude doesn't work in the marriage, except maybe in the beginning. In "The Road Less Traveled," Scott Peck says the falling-in-love phase, complete with romantic moments, is crucial for couples. Later in the relationship, the couple may have to remember those moments to get through difficult times. But the blissful I-finally-found-someone period doesn't last. As it shouldn't. A mature relationship needs to look outward as much as inward. To grow, a couple must fulfill its role within a community.

I suspect that's the way it's always been. In tribal times, people paired up, but they didn't go live in a hut all by themselves. They were a unit within a larger context.

In my own experience, the community has played a crucial role in sustaining our almost 20-year relationship. Friends have fed us, watched our kids, listened to our problems, given us books, even cleaned our dirty kitchen during a particularly trying time. One friend, after listening to both Terry and me rant separately about a problem we were having, said, "You guys need to go to a marriage counselor." Then she placed in our hands the phone number of a good therapist.

A good community can help defuse anger, offer options, lend a hand, provide resources, supply role models, make us laugh, share in our joys and successes. But none of this can happen if the relationship is seen as "private," if no one ever knows what's going on, if few people ever cross over your threshold.

A red flag goes up every time I hear about a couple who rarely go out, who are isolated, who say, "Keep away — this is none of your business."

Being connected to a community isn't a panacea. Even if you're well-connected, your marriage may still fall apart. But if you let the community in, it has a better chance of survival.

So I think it was great that my friends let a lot of people celebrate their union. Their marriage isn't just about them. It involves all of us.

Jan. 7, 2003

Be thankful for the righteous among us

The world, according to Jewish legend, is maintained by the Lamed Vav — 36 righteous men. (Lamed and vav are Hebrew letters that numerically represent 36.)

A distinguishing characteristic of these folks, however, is that they're hidden. They're often poor and unknown, and even they don't know they're lamedvavniks. (Given that women's work is so hidden, I suspect a good number of them are actually female.) When one dies, another is born. But without all 36, the world would end.

Despite their anonymity, however, I think I might have met a few. They weren't drawing attention to themselves — that would disqualify them right there. But when I inadvertently learned of their work, I grew suspicious.

One man took in stray dogs that he discovered while delivering Meals on Wheels. His wife said he just couldn't overlook these starving creatures. In the midst of one good deed, he does another.

A woman with Lou Gehrig's disease can't move or even speak. But she gets other people to pack up baby clothes for a teenage mother she knows.

Several people go down to the Capitol rotunda at noon the day after each Florida execution. They can't change anybody's mind at this point. They're not protesting or blaming anyone. They just bear witness to the life of the victim *and* the Death Row inmate. No great fanfare. Just a moment of humanness.

I suspect these people are lamedvavniks because of the deep gratitude that wells up in me when I find out what they've done. They aren't trying to win community service points. They aren't angling for the cameras. They just do what they do because it's needed.

That's how the righteous hold up the world.

But I'll never know whether any of these people is the real McCoy. An accurate determination would let the rest of us off the hook. As long as the lamedvavniks do their work, why should we worry?

But what if *you* are a lamedvavnik? What if *I* am? Our very actions could save the world or destroy it.

Now that's a Jewish guilt trip.

Rabbi Rami Shapiro, a meditation teacher and author of "Minyan," has started a Lamed Vav Project (www.simply-jewish.com) to help us out. He said the rabbis knew that people couldn't be righteous all the time, so they interpreted the Lamed Vav to mean that *at any given moment* 36 people in the world are acting righteously. We could take turns.

Shapiro suggests picking a day of the week when the rest of the world can count on you to act righteously. We should do this all the time, he said, but especially so on this day. If enough people do it, the world won't collapse.

On the other days, keep your eyes peeled. Lamedvavniks can pop up anywhere. They might be next door, at your child's school, in your place of worship. If you suspect you've found one, don't say anything. Don't give her away. Just close your eyes and whisper, "Thanks."

Jan. 21, 2003

Abortion is a thorny issue for us all

The January anniversary of Roe v. Wade, the Supreme Court case legalizing abortion, brought up the "yuck factor" for me.

Paying attention to the y-factor is a skill I try to teach my children: If something makes you feel yucky inside, it's probably wrong.

But as a feminist, I haven't wanted to look too closely at abortion. Reproductive rights seem essential for women. Many of my friends have had abortions. I don't want to be judgmental.

But the yuck feeling just won't go away.

Mostly I question whether saying that abortion is a "private" decision serves us well. The older I get, the more I realize that few, if any, decisions are truly private. We are all part of a vast web, and the slightest movement on that web produces endless ripples in the world as well as in our souls.

Abortion is not exempt. Early in my reporting career, pro-choice folks had a news conference at which several women talked about having an abortion and how it was the right choice for them. When I asked the organizers whether they had ever talked to women who had regretted the decision, they cut me off. We weren't going to discuss *that*. And I wondered: Why not? Why can't women who feel good about their decision and women who feel bad be in the same room? What's the danger?

Opinions on abortion are so polarized that women often keep the decision to themselves. Like men who come back from war and seldom talk about their battle experiences, women rarely talk about their abortions, even to their closest friends. Should a woman, years after her abortion, find herself obsessing about her unborn child, having frequent nightmares or weeping at pictures of embryos because she now wants to get pregnant, where can she go? Some churches may offer counseling, but my guess is that most women suffer in silence.

And what about the man? What if he has a change of heart? We rarely hear about the long-term effect on him.

That's why I would never advise a woman, particularly a young woman, to get an abortion. What she does today may seem like the right decision; 10 or 15 years down the road, though, it may flip to the other side. If she suddenly feels it's wrong, there's no way to right it.

Making abortion a private decision gets the rest of us off the hook. *Our* hands stay clean. We can push it to the back of our minds.

My mother, a vehement pro-lifer, can't. To her, abortion is murder. So she spends hours talking about chastity to eighth-graders in her large Catholic church in South Florida.

For years, abortion was such a hot topic in our family — I was on one side, my mom and sisters were on the other — that we agreed not to discuss it. But I have to say that my mother has done more to prevent abortions than I ever have.

In fact, I haven't done a thing. Because I've subscribed to the "private decision" line, I haven't gotten involved.

Instead, I'm stuck in my yuckness. I still don't want abortions to be outlawed. However difficult and long-range the decision is, I don't want the government telling a woman that she *must* have that child. I agree with pro-choice folks who say that will only lead to botched back-alley abortions. Forcing a woman to maintain a pregnancy is not the answer.

On the other hand, I'm grateful for those who take the opposite position, pulling the web in the other direction. If they didn't raise their voices in protest, I fear we'd all become cavalier, dispensing with the fetus as just so much tissue rather than as the potential life it is. What kind of world would that be?

We need passionate people on both sides of this issue. Perhaps in the tension created between them, we can move one step closer to moral ground.

Feb. 18, 2003

His focus on peace hasn't wavered

Today William Coombs will walk into the Federal Prison Camp at Eglin Air Force Base carrying an identification card, some cash and a Bible with the addresses of his loved ones written in the back. He'll be there for three months.

His crime: protesting at a U.S. military base.

But before you jump to conclusions, let me tell you that his focus isn't Iraq — it's Latin America.

For decades, a school at Fort Benning, Ga., has taught combat training to people from Latin and South America in hopes that these countries could help fight terrorism, stop illegal drug trafficking and respond to disasters. Unfortunately, some graduates have terrorized their own people instead.

Manuel Noriega is a graduate. So are the soldiers who massacred Jesuit priests in El Salvador. So are the Colombian military leaders accused of social cleansing.

The list goes on. (See www.soaw.org.)

It makes Coombs sick. In November, at an annual protest at Fort Benning, he trespassed onto the base property and was promptly arrested.

Originally, I thought his action was futile. With the country's attention riveted on Iraq, who would want to hear about Latin America?

But Coombs, a Vietnam veteran and retired Tallahassee schoolteacher, is one of the long-haulers. Those of us with shorter attention spans have a hard time understanding them.

They latch onto things. They don't let go, even when the winds of popular opinion change. They hang onto their vision.

Coombs became interested in Central America more than 20 years ago. While he was visiting Nicaragua in 1988, Contra soldiers ambushed a boat he was on. Two people died and numerous others were wounded, including a man less than a foot away from Coombs.

Instead of being frightened, he became more resolved to help the people in that region.

For 10 years he collected school supplies from Ruediger Elementary, where he worked, and sent them to poor communities in Latin America. He worked with groups such as Pastors for Peace and Witness for Peace. He educated himself about international economics. He helped build a rural school in Panama. In 2001, he visited Nicaragua again. Although some things had improved — people were more literate, for instance — health care was still abysmal.

When he got back, he wanted to deepen his commitment. He had heard of the annual November protests at The School of the Americas (now renamed the Western Hemisphere Institute for Security Cooperation) at Fort Benning, but he had never gone. This year, he was determined to go.

He didn't plan on getting arrested. Most of the protesters there didn't. They came just for the solemn funeral procession where names of people massacred by graduates of the school were read aloud.

But being there, knowing he wasn't alone, emboldened him. The next day, along with several dozen other people, he trespassed on the edge of government property.

It didn't matter that most Americans were focused on Saddam Hussein. The timing was right for him.

Coombs knows his arrest — and his stay in jail — won't change the world. But during a benefit for him a few months ago, he was able to educate 300 people about the school at Fort Benning. There've been a few articles in the paper about him. He hopes to talk about his experience after he gets out of prison.

For this long-hauler, that's more than enough.

April 8, 2003

Older and wiser, I now know to savor life

I'm sitting in the shade of an oak tree. I smell the spring air. The sun is brilliant. My 11-month-old daughter, who is crawling over my legs, looks up and grins, jutting out her lower jaw with its two teeth and crinkling her nose.

What a piece of heaven.

No one needs to tell me to stop and smell the roses. I already do. I'm a mom in my 40s.

This week I talked with two other older moms and we all agreed: It doesn't get better than this. True, we're tired. Yes, we're sometimes mistaken for grandmothers. And more than once I've joked: When Jenna graduates from high school, Terry and I are going straight into assisted living.

But right now I'm very patient. I'm not fretting about my career. I know that the sleepless nights will end, that the teething stage is but a blip. I'm not rushing to get through anything.

When my oldest son, now 14, was a baby, I was always looking ahead. I wanted to accomplish things, be productive. I grew restless being with an infant all day. I counted the days until I felt I could put him in day care so I could enter the "real" world again.

Now I know that it doesn't get realer than being with those you love.

Age may not make you wiser, but it can give you perspective. When I was pregnant with David, five of my friends agreed to be on my birth team. Since then, three of them have had breast cancer.

Though they're all surviving well, cancer has now taken up permanent residence in my consciousness. I keep waiting for another shoe to drop, for another friend to get it. And then one does. This year, two more friends got the dreaded diagnosis.

I never thought about cancer, or death, when David was little. But with Jenna, I think about it every day. I make elaborate plans in my head about what I'd do if Terry or I had to get chemotherapy. I push myself to exercise, even when I'm tired, because I don't want to lose any bone mass. I agree to eat fake butter on my popcorn to keep my cholesterol levels low.

But the upside is that, with each milestone Jenna passes — sitting up by herself, clapping for the first time, picking up a carrot with her thumb and index finger — I'm filled with a sweet gratitude for being alive to see it. I don't let myself get distracted. I pay attention. More than ever, I'm in the present moment.

So let the younger moms run around, trying to do it all. Sitting under the oak tree with Jenna is all I need.

April 15, 2003

Worlds unfold outside the front door

Last night, I saw the fireflies. I was on a walk just about dusk, trudging up a hill after leaving my boisterous kids at home. Suddenly, I was surrounded by dozens of twinkling lights.

The air got cooler. The sky darkened. I stood still.

When I started walking again, I found other patches, lights blinking and swirling, diamonds in the dark. I later learned that this is the best time to see them, late April to early May, and that the males are the ones flying around flashing — the females hang out on the ground.

I should have known this already. I've lived in the neighborhood 12 years. Yet before last night, I never really saw them.

Sometimes we don't see what's right beneath our noses.

I have been a little wistful lately about my lack of adventure. Over the years I've read a steady stream of books about women who have climbed in the Himalayas, kayaked around Lake Superior, gone to the North Pole, built cabins in the Arctic, walked across Tibet, sailed solo around the world. I knew I'd never break any records, but I always thought I had some of their spirit, that someday I'd venture out into the wilderness by myself.

Instead, life decision after life decision has kept me homebound. I rarely leave Tallahassee. Since my 1-year-old daughter was born, half-hour walks around the neighborhood are about all the adventure I get.

Yet that may be enough.

Jewish tradition teaches that there are four levels to interpreting the Torah. First, there's the simple or literal meaning of the story. Then there's the allegorical, or hinted at, meaning. Next, there's the pursued meaning, in which you might have to dissect a Hebrew word or see where else it's used in the Torah to understand the passage. Finally, there's the hidden or mystical meaning. All four levels are there all the time. The reader may dip into one and then, at another time of life, dip into another. But knowing that all those layers are there makes tackling the Torah challenging and exciting.

When I saw the fireflies as if for the first time, I was reminded that there are also many levels to the world. Even ground you have covered, over and over again, can yield up new things, fresh insights. You just have to go deeper.

I thought I knew my neighborhood. I had it down pat. And then I was introduced to a whole new dance of light — magic, on the same old road.

April 29, 2003

Heart of a nomad beats within this mom

"Tales of a Female Nomad."

The title draws me like a magnet.

I can't even make it out of Dodge, let alone sell my belongings and head for the open road. Three kids. A partner. A job. A house. It just doesn't fit into the schedule.

But at night in my dreams, I'm weightless. The family is gone. I'm young again and I'm floating down rivers, trekking up mountains, seeing strange, colorful, beautiful birds. I walk down dark, abandoned roads. I get tossed in gigantic waves. I lie on a mountaintop, the wind blowing across my body, my heart opening wider and wider to the blue sky.

Then the baby cries and I wake with a start.

Rita Golden Gelman's book, then, is a little gift from heaven. I greedily read about how she starts a whole new life for herself in her late 40s after the kids are grown and her marriage dissolves. She sets out to see the world, no particular plan in mind. She sleeps with sea lions in the Galapagos Islands and observes orangutans in the rain forest of Borneo; she makes *gallo pinto*, a bean-and-rice dish, with a woman in Nicaragua and participates in a cremation ceremony with the *banjar*, a community bound by religion and custom, in Bali.

I'm barely through the book when Marybeth Bond breezes into town. Bond has written five books on women and travel, including "Gutsy Women" and "A Woman's World." She speaks at a fundraising luncheon for Refuge House, regaling the 100-plus women in the audience with tales of female adventures. There's the battered woman who ends up climbing Mount Everest and the 68-year-old grandmother who tubes down the Colorado River rapids. There's her own story of going to Bangkok by herself at 29, even though she'd never gone out to dinner or to a movie by herself.

Her advice: Don't let fear stop you.

"The purpose is not to rid your stomach of the butterflies," she said, "but to make them fly in formation."

I laugh when I read on her website that the average adventure traveler is not a 28-year-old male — it's a 47-year-old female. *And she wears a size 12 dress.*

Yippee!

Young people, she said, travel to find themselves. Older folks want to *lose* themselves.

And it's never too late.

Bond has written another book: "Gutsy Mamas: Travel Tips and Wisdom for Mothers on the Road." I'm ordering it today.

This summer, by golly, those butterflies are going to fly.

May 13, 2003

Fashion keeps a shackle on women

When I became a feminist 25 years ago, I was sure that high heels would go the way of separate water fountains for whites and blacks. They'd be anachronisms relegated to museums. When my daughter saw the barely-bigger-than-a-toothpick heels, she'd shake her head and ask, "Women actually wore those, Mom?"

I'd sigh and say, "Yes, dear. Can you believe it?"

Instead, those heels are alive and flourishing, crowding out every comfortable shoe in sight besides sneakers and a few sandals. When I went shopping recently for a flat work shoe that was slightly more stylish than nurses' footwear, I was out of luck. Even the ones that had low heels were flimsy, or the toe was too pointed, or the heel narrowed down to the size of a quarter.

After all these years, I thought I'd have more options.

Now, I know there's a decent shoe out there somewhere, but it's mighty hard to find. Instead, I'm bombarded with row after row of ugly, torturous shoes that seem bent on making women wobble.

The worst part is that, unlike the blacks who were forced to use separate water fountains, women *choose* to wear these things. In fact, if anybody gets mad at me about this column, I bet it won't be a man. They might like high heels, but if women wanted to chuck them to be more comfortable, I think they'd understand.

It's women who are driving this. Why? To be sexy? To be stylish?

I think wearing high heels succeeds in doing only one thing: projecting vulnerability.

In so many ways, women have made tremendous advances in a very short time. We stampeded into colleges, grabbed control of our sexuality, pushed for every right under the sun. When I talk with young women today, I marvel at their confidence. They take on challenges I never even dreamed of at their age.

But when it comes to fashion, they're more shackled than ever.

We're supposed to be reed-thin, flat-bellied and high-heeled. The result: a beauty standard that is as rigid as at any other time in history.

This is freedom?

Ladies, we could end this today. Nobody could stop us. I can see us now, a whole movement of flat-footed women — steady on our feet, keeping pace, striding confidently across the land.

May 27, 2003

Remember, you look marvelous!

According to a *Newsweek* article, 90 percent of men are happy with the way they look.

Ninety percent? Amazing.

If women said the same thing, it'd be front-page news. But that would never happen. Finding even one woman who liked her appearance would be an accomplishment.

The same week I read the *Newsweek* article, I got an item in the mail from Denise Austin, a fitness expert. "Shrink Your Female Fat Zones," shrieked the cover.

How did she know I'd need this? Did she have spies searching for potential customers? "There's one! She needs a little shrinkage. Write her name down!"

No way. The assumption is that every woman has a zone problem.

Most also have an aging problem. But according to *Newsweek*, half of men aren't worried about aging "at all." If they could change one thing about their appearance, only 4 percent said they'd want a younger face.

Oh, that women could say the same things. What would the world be like?

We'd get up in the morning, take a quick shower, dry our hair and brush our teeth. As we walked out the door, we'd glance in the mirror and say, "Lookin' good!"

At lunchtime we'd eat whatever we wanted. If we bumped into an old friend, our arms wouldn't fold over our stomachs. We'd talk with our mother for an entire hour without once mentioning weight.

At the beach we'd stand, arms akimbo, looking out to sea. We'd go straight for the larger sizes in the clothing stores without a bit of embarrassment. In grocery stores, we wouldn't even notice the low-fat labels.

We'd stand taller. Spread our arms wider. Laugh a whole lot more.

Those wrinkles around the eyes? They make us look distinguished. That added weight around the hips? Doesn't hurt a thing. Brown spots on our hands? Nobody'll notice those.

No more magazine stories about how great Demi Moore looks at 40. No more botox parties. No more trying to look 15 when we're actually 45. *No more fat zones!*

Just one big 90-percent-happy zone. Equal rights in the looks department.

July 22, 2003

I am, like many Americans, filthy stinking rich

I couldn't look. It was obscene. But my son insisted.

A $900,000 watch.

He pulled the magazine away in amazement. At 14, he's excited about "things." Lamborghinis. Mansions. Yachts. Often he has talked about things he'd get if he became rich.

I tell myself that it's just his age. That he'll outgrow it. That he'd never, ever wear anything that cost nearly a million dollars.

"What's wrong with making money?" he wants to know.

I try to give him perspective. After dinner a few days later, in one of my parental "teaching moments," I read him a story from the *Democrat* about a group of college students who took part in a hunger banquet. Some students represented the majority of the world's population — 55 percent — who earn $755 or less a year. They were given rice to eat with their hands. The next group, representing another 30 percent, got rice and beans. Only the last group — a mere 15 percent who earn more than $9,265 a year — got a full-course meal including chicken and dessert.

The story gave me pause. Compared with most of the world, I'm already wearing million-dollar clothes.

I like to think I'm not materialistic. But don't take away my morning coffee, my chocolate, my books. I'd never sell my car, move to a smaller house, give up vacations. I want my kids to have music lessons, get a good education.

Am I willing to give up any of that so others can have more? Not really.

I'm willing to do more for others, but I don't want to do without. Yet I know that if this gross imbalance in the world is ever going to change, we rich folks will have to let go of some goods.

What will my contribution be?

After I finished reading the article aloud, nobody said anything. My son left the table. But in a few minutes he was back.

"Mom, some people are hungry their *whole* life," he said, grimacing. "They're hungry all day. I don't like to be hungry more than two hours."

Neither do I. We sat there, bellies full, trying to imagine what that would be like.

We didn't have a clue.

Aug. 12, 2003

Watching with trepidation as friends lose their parents

Almost every week for the last six months, someone I know has lost a parent.

This one from a sudden heart attack. That one from cancer. Another with Alzheimer's.

Every time one dies, the next generation moves up a notch. Some of my friends are now the oldest ones in their families.

I like to think that I won't be joining them anytime soon. My parents are only in their late 60s.

But my days are numbered. I can feel it in my bones every time another parent passes.

As a result, I'm hypervigilant. When I visit my parents, I imagine that this will be the last time we get together. If they say or do something that upsets me, I ignore it. Petty disagreements won't mean a thing should they suddenly die the next week. Our last interaction, I'm determined, is going to be positive.

I also try to imagine what life will be like without them. Not much different on the outside. I've lived away from them all of my adult life.

But the inside is another matter. Even though I'm very different from them, they're still role models for me, both positively and negatively. "I want to be like that" or "I *don't* want to be like that." Just as when I was an adolescent (and

I see my own teenager doing this with me now), we're in a tug of war, pulling against one another. They force me one step forward, I yank them two steps back.

When they're no longer there, the rope will suddenly go slack. I'm bound to fall down, at least for a while.

For many people, it's hard to imagine living past the age that their parents died. My life partner, whose mother died at age 58, said it's like looking out over a vast wilderness, with not a clue about which way to go.

I'm grateful that my parents are still alive to give me hints about what's out there. I try to pay attention, to honor their wisdom, to show my love and appreciation.

I want my kids to know them, too, so I never skip the summer visit or holiday get-together. When I'm on the phone with them I'll ask my kids, "Want to talk to Grandma?"

Because someday I'll get the call: "Mom's in the hospital." "Dad's had a heart attack." "Sherry, come home."

I've watched it happen with one friend after another. They pack their bags. They bring Mom to town or visit Dad every weekend. They talk with doctors and figure out insurance. They hold their parent's hand. They say goodbye.

Afterward, they have a new look in their eyes. Some are more tender. Others make radical life changes. A few just cry more easily.

No one is the same.

Aug. 26, 2003

Required giving misses important point

The first time my 14-year-old son asked that his volunteer work be documented, I winced.

I know his school requires it — and so will any scholarships he might apply for — but getting credit for community service?

Doesn't seem right.

Sure, there are benefits. The students get more involved in the community. The community improves. What starts out as a duty might turn into a lifelong passion. I recently heard of a boy who grudgingly agreed to play his violin at a nursing home only to find out he loved doing it.

But allowing kids to rack up volunteer hours like so many poker chips may backfire. I remember interviewing a young woman years ago who told me about volunteer work she was doing. My interest immediately was piqued. Finding out why she was involved would give me insight into her character. But instead of being motivated by some heart-rending story in the newspaper, some tragedy of someone close to her or a compulsion to help others, she said, "Well, you know, the Bright Futures Scholarship requires that you do 75 hours of community service."

So much for your right hand not knowing what your left hand is doing, as Jesus suggested.

In the 12th century, Jewish philosopher Moses Maimonides ranked eight ways of giving *tzedakah* (which literally means justice, but is more popularly known as charity). The highest form of *tzedakah* is giving in a way that allows someone to no longer need *tzedakah*. But the lower forms, in ascending order, are:

- Giving reluctantly.
- Giving less than you should, but giving graciously.
- Giving what you should, but only after being asked.
- Giving before being asked.
- Giving without knowing the recipient, but the recipient knowing you.
- Giving knowing the recipient, but without the recipient knowing you.
- Giving completely anonymously.

I wonder where "Giving for scholarship credit" would fall on his scale.

Don't get me wrong. I always feel puffed up when I do something good for someone. I feel even *better* when other people know about it.

But the goal — and one I hope we project for our children — is anonymous giving.

It reminds me of the story of Yosele the Holy Miser. Yosele was known throughout the town as a stingy person, even though he was wealthy. Beggars steered clear of him because he would berate anyone who approached him. Even the rabbi talked negatively about him.

When he died, no one came to his funeral. He received a pauper's burial, just a hole in the ground. But the Friday morning after he died, the town beggars poured into the rabbi's house. They complained that they hadn't received an envelope with money tucked in their door the way they had every Friday morning for years.

After pondering the problem for hours, they decided the only person who could have been the anonymous donor was Yosele.

Later that night, the rabbi had a dream about Yosele, who was in heaven. The rabbi apologized for speaking so badly about him.

"What can I do for you, Yosele?" he asked.

Yosele said he didn't need anything. Heaven was perfect. Except for one thing.

"I don't get the feeling I used to get before sunrise on Friday mornings when I delivered those envelopes. That time is over for me now. I just want you to know that there are some things even more important than heaven!"

We may turn our children into good citizens by requiring community service. But if we can learn — and then teach our children — to give anonymously, we can transform our souls.

Oct. 7, 2003

Sharing Mom's wheels could be cool

The pestering started a year and a half ago, as soon as David turned 13.

"What kind of car are you going to get me when I'm 16?" he'd ask, all eager and bright-eyed.

"You're not going to get a car, David," I'd respond. "You *might* have access to my car."

I don't know why, but he didn't believe me. He thought I must be kidding. Surely I wouldn't expect him to actually drive a cobalt-blue, 1994 Taurus *station wagon*. Or our other car, a dark green Toyota *van*. Those were Mommobiles.

Sorry, buddy. That's as good as it gets.

So he'd try to hit up Terry, thinking he'd have a better chance with her. She was noncommittal: "We'll talk."

That only gave him hope. When I told him for the hundredth time that he wasn't getting a car, he'd say, "Oh, I know what you're doing. You're going to keep saying no, but on my 16th birthday you'll hand me the keys to my new car. You want to surprise me."

Oy vey.

What he didn't seem to understand was that money isn't the problem (although it surely factors in). Nor am I concerned about giving him wheels — he's been nothing but mature and levelheaded all his life.

For me, getting a third car is a moral issue.

Most of us don't like to frame our purchases in such terms. If we have the money, we can buy anything we want. Guilt-free. It's our *right*. Nothing more fundamental than that.

But we have to draw the line somewhere, and I draw a line on a third car. Here's why.

- ♦ **The environment.** The biggest cause of global warming is the burning of fossil fuels. We don't like to think about that when we're driving around in our cars, but every trip adds to this mushrooming problem. Members of the local group Heart of the Earth, environmentalists focused on this Red Hills region, say reducing consumption of fossil fuels is the No. 1 thing an individual can do to save the earth. Recycling, which is so hyped in the media and elsewhere, is really just peanuts compared with what one person can do by not using — or not buying — a car.
- ♦ **Materialism.** Let's face it, we don't need a third car. Maybe not even a second. We live within a mile of the high school, the mall, both Terry's and my jobs. It's just about convenience. As a tiny sign of solidarity with most of the world's people — who make less than $1,000 a year and barely have enough to eat — we can surely not get a third vehicle.
- ♦ **Slower lifestyle.** Adding another car would just increase the busyness of our lives. We'd go more places, zipping here and there, because we could. But we don't need more motion in our lives — we need more stillness. If we have to share, there'll be times I won't have the car, times David won't. We might just have to walk, take a bus, not go.

I explained this one night to Terry while we sat on the back porch. She was silent for a few moments.

"I didn't realize *that's* why you didn't want him to have a car."

Later, she tried to explain it to David. Not long afterward, he started redesigning the Taurus. We can get a flame painted on the hood, he said. We can add a fancy stereo system with speakers in the back. We can get leather seat covers and shiny new hubcaps. To get started, he even washed the car last week without being asked.

"This might not be so bad," he allowed. "It might even be kind of cool."

"Yeah," I agreed, my relief turning to giddiness. I might even buy him a pair of fuzzy dice to hang from the mirror of my Mommobile.

Nov. 18, 2003

Tooth fairy may vanish, but she'll be back

We don't talk much about Santa Claus since we're Jewish, but I figured my 8-year-old son knew the score. A mother had complained to me a couple of years ago that Noah was telling her son what the real deal was. He'd have a similar take on the tooth fairy, I was sure.

I was wrong.

When he lost his first tooth well into his seventh year, the tooth fairy wrote him a note the first night explaining why she was late getting him his present (it was something special and wasn't ready yet). He didn't blink an eye. Even though the handwriting was strikingly familiar, he remained a staunch believer.

A couple of weeks ago, he surprised me again. When he was young, his stuffed animals would come out and play in his room — *if* his room was clean. When he'd wake up in the morning, his Pooh Bear, raccoon and turtle might be sitting in a circle playing cards or driving his trucks. Terry said the same thing had happened to her stuffed animals when she was a kid. Her mother told her that they'd start playing as soon as she fell asleep, but the minute she woke up, they'd freeze in place.

Well, over Thanksgiving, Noah's room was clean for the first time in months (grandparents were coming, after all), and the animals came out to play. He'd bring all of us into his room in the morning to show us their latest antics. But my 14-year-old son wouldn't play along.

"You know who really does this," David said, grinning mischievously at Noah. "It's really Ima." ("Ima" is "Mom" in Hebrew.)

Noah blinked a couple of times and looked up at me. "Is it, Mom? Is it really you guys?"

I was noncommittal (after shooting David an if-looks-could-kill glance), but I thought Noah surely got it. Again, I was wrong.

The next morning he happily dragged his grandparents into his room to show them how the animals had broken into his money jar.

I can't blame him for not wanting to let go. Fantasy can bring out the best in us.

So I'm not in any hurry for Noah to face up to reality. The magic of a present under his pillow and of animals that frolic at night makes him laugh. Terry gets a certain look in her eye, too — remembering her mother, who died before our children were born.

I know the animals will grow still as Noah gets older. But I won't be too sad. Years from now, when my grand-children's rooms are clean, I'm sure they'll come out again to play.

Dec. 9, 2003

Religion is a ripe subject for Hollywood

Mel Gibson's movie, "The Passion," that opened last week makes me realize I'm hungry.

Not for Bible stories per se. Not for a "biblically correct" script.

But just for popular culture to take religion seriously.

I racked my brain trying to think of a modern movie or book that explored the main character's religious life. Perhaps a character questions his or her faith, or changes it, or loses it. Or maybe a character actually prays to God for guidance or wonders, "What would God think?"

OK, maybe a few such popular works are out there, but let's face it: I wouldn't be so starved if religious themes were dealt with even 10 percent as much as the trite love story, the boring action flick, the overcoming-the-odds film, the sex-for-the-sake-of-sex and violence-for-the-sake-of-violence blockbuster — of even, for Pete's sake, the old reliable *dog* movie.

I'm not interested in pat answers. But many people, every day, grapple with deep religious issues.

You'd just never know it from Hollywood.

The one piece of literature I can remember that dealt seriously with religion was "The Brothers Karamazov," written by the great Russian novelist Fyodor Dostoevsky more than a century ago. The story focuses on three brothers and their father. Central to the plot is how each brother relates — or doesn't relate — to God. One believes. One doesn't. One isn't sure.

They all have faults and all make terrible mistakes, but their beliefs about God define who they are and determine their fate.

I read the book almost 20 years ago, long before I considered myself a religious person. One scene still stands out vividly in my mind. The youngest brother, Alyosha, is having a spiritual crisis. The faith of his youth is called into question. Among other things, he overhears someone reading the Gospels, specifically the story about Jesus at the wedding at Cana. It was the site of Jesus' first miracle. He didn't heal somebody. He didn't bring somebody back to life. He just brought *happiness* to a group of poor people.

Something in the story stirs Alyosha's soul. Overcome with emotion, he rushes outside and drops to the ground. I recently looked up the passage:

He did not know why he was hugging the earth, why he could not kiss it enough, why he longed to kiss it all. He kissed it again and again, drenching it with his tears, vowing to love it always, always. "Water the earth with the tears of your joy and love those tears," a voice rang out in his soul. . . . It was as if the threads of all those innumerable words of God had met in his soul and his soul was vibrating. . . . He craved to forgive everyone and everything and to beg for forgiveness. . . . He was a weak youth when he fell on the ground and he rose a strong and determined fighter. He knew it. He felt it during that moment of rapture. And never, never thereafter would Alyosha forget that moment. "Someone visited my soul then," he would say later.

I don't need to see Jesus or saints up on the big screen. I want ordinary people struggling with 21st-century religious questions. How do we maintain our faith when exposed to other world religions? How do we synthesize our need for rationality with our desire for transcendence? How do interfaith couples raise religious children? How do women find a place in patriarchal religion? How do we pray when the traditional words fail us?

Even something simple would do: a moment of rapture, an awakening, when God touches our soul and we grab the earth in ecstasy.

March 2, 2004

Sharing the load: From laundry to parenting duties

What's the name and phone number of your child's pediatrician? When was the last time you sorted through your child's old clothes or toys? How much lead time do you need to set up a kid's haircut appointment, to send out invitations for a birthday party or to cancel a piano lesson without penalty?

Most moms know the answers. Many dads may not.

It's one reason author Karen Bouris wrote "Just Kiss Me and Tell Me You Did the Laundry: How to Negotiate Equal Roles for Husband and Wife in Parenting, Career, and Home Life."

I can sympathize.

But it ain't my problem.

My lesbian partner and I don't need a book to help us traverse this tricky terrain. Equal parenting comes naturally.

In all this hoopla over gay marriage — and how it will or won't harm straight couples — one thing has been overlooked: Lesbian parents can be *role models*.

Don't get me wrong. Lesbian couples have the same problems that straight ones do — power struggles and nasty breakups, meddling in-laws and back-talking kids. We argue about money and sex and what to do on vacation.

But housework and parenting? It's assumed both people will carry that load.

Terry knows the pediatrician's number, but it's a flip of the coin who takes the kids to their appointments. I sort through the old clothes, but Terry buys them shoes and gets them haircuts. I do the laundry and the shopping (because I work part time), but she's the one who goes through the backpacks and fills out all those school forms; organizes the stuff to take on family trips; RSVPs for everything from birthday parties to school functions; and never forgets when the tooth fairy is supposed to come.

In her next edition, I hope Bouris includes a chapter on gay parents — and how they work out who does what. Her readers might find it illuminating.

Of course, all of us could use a little improvement.

A couple of years ago we ended up in the emergency room when one of our boys had a nasty gash on his knee. The doctor came up to us, clipboard in hand.

"Which one is the mother?" he asked.

"We both are," Terry answered.

He made a note with his pen and then asked: "When was his last tetanus shot?"

I looked at Terry. Terry looked at me. The doctor didn't miss a beat:

"Two moms and you don't know when his last tetanus shot was?"

March 23, 2004

Suffering people need more than compassion

I'm sitting in Barnes & Noble with my cafe latte, ready for a nice Sunday-afternoon break. I unfold *The New York Times* and take a sip of coffee, already starting to relax.

That's when I see her.

She's in a picture on the bottom of the front page. She's on her side, naked, her head resting on her mother's thigh. One of her rod-thin legs is bent up toward her stomach.

But it's her jaw line that gets me. Her teeth are clenched and her bottom lip protrudes just a bit. I instinctively want to run my finger along her jaw, from ear to chin. She reminds me of my own 2-year-old daughter.

What did the mother say to this little girl of indeterminate age, who was born in Sudan and forced to leave her home because of civil war? She's starving. The paper said the children are so weak they don't even cry.

Those of us who follow the news at all are subject to a steady stream of such horrifying images. Wounded children. AIDS victims. Orphans. Sometimes it hits us in the gut, brings tears to our eyes.

But then we move on.

We don't lack compassion. Other people's suffering bothers us. What we lack is *urgency*.

When it comes to our own kids, we make sure they have the best and take advantage of every opportunity. Even when we're dead tired, even when we don't really have the time or money, we make sure we go to those school functions, buy those Christmas presents, traipse all over kingdom come so they can participate in sports, drama, music.

Work in behalf of others, particularly those on the other side of the world, well, that can often wait. Since November, I've had an idea about how to raise money for a project run by the American Jewish World Service. The organization, among other things, provides small business loans to women in the developing world. Sometimes the loans are as small as $50, just enough to buy a cow or a few chickens. The program, like similar microfinancing ones run by other agencies, is very successful. Often more than 90 percent of the women pay back the loan — and then become eligible for a larger one.

I'd like to say that I just haven't had the time to help out. But that's not exactly true — it's how I've chosen to spend my time. I tend to pour most of my energy into me and mine. The birthday parties to plan, the weeklong vacation at the beach, the effort to get my older son to and from a month-long summer camp. I've seen my share of movies, gone to plenty of parties, read lots of books.

I have the time.

What needs to happen is that the rumbling in someone's stomach half a world away needs to affect me — at least to some degree — the way my own kids' hunger does. Then there'd be no pussyfooting around.

I look at the girl's picture again. My daughter lies on my lap, just like this child on her mother's lap. The curve of her head, the delicate ear, so similar. I can almost hear her breathing.

I vow to start my fundraising project. Today.

July 27, 2004

Anger and love surge in family storms

My family presents well. The kids are bright and cheerful. We laugh and hug a lot. Many people comment that we're just so, well, *healthy.*

Few of them saw us several weeks ago.

As Hurricanes Frances and Ivan whirled toward us for days on end, we had our own storm brewing. Lots of yelling, slamming doors, tears of frustration. More than once I thought, "Whatever possessed me to think that I could be a parent?"

One thing that gave me hope was not something out of a parenting book, but out of a bestseller called "The Seven Principles for Making Marriage Work" by John M. Gottman. In the book, Gottman says that couples in healthy marriages often fight as much as those in unhealthy ones. I was stunned when I read this.

But he went on to say that neither the number— nor the volume — of arguments mattered as much as what he called "repair attempts." These were actions or words that one spouse would do or say to defuse a situation. In the midst of a heated quarrel, for instance, the wife might suddenly make a funny face. If the husband started laughing, the tension was reduced, and their connection was reaffirmed. If the husband ignored the attempt and went on with the argument, that spelled trouble, Gottman said.

I figured the same thing was probably true with parents and children. Even healthy families fight a lot. Loudly. There never seems to be a shortage of things to squabble about. But if we can try, over and over again, to repair the breaches, we'll be OK.

I started looking for those "repair attempts," particularly with my middle child. One happened in a formal way. On Rosh Hashanah, the day Hurricane Ivan hit the Panhandle, we were at Lake Ella for *tashlich*, the Jewish New Year ritual of casting our sins into a body of water. After our rabbi said the appropriate prayers, everyone was supposed to take bread crumbs — representing our sins — and toss them into the lake.

My middle child stood holding his piece of bread. He apologized for the way he'd been acting. Then he looked at me. Didn't I have anything to say? The anger that had been lodged in my throat for the past few weeks lessened a little. Yes, I was sorry, too. He looked at me seriously and said, "I forgive you."

Our crumbs were barely in the water before the ducks gobbled them up.

The other repair attempt was more spontaneous. It was one night when I was furious with my son and ordered him to take a shower and go directly to his room. Not long after, I was putting my 2-year-old daughter to sleep in the crib. The room was dark except for the light from the hallway that filtered through the half-closed door. I rubbed her back as I sang her a lullaby from an old Cris Williamson album: *Like a ship in the harbor, like a mother and child, like a light in the darkness, I'll hold you a while.*

As I started the second stanza, I heard my son on the other side of the door joining in: *We'll rock on the water,*

I'll cradle you deep, and watch while the angels sing you to sleep.

I stood by my daughter's bed for a few seconds, a strange stirring in my chest.

When I walked out of the room, my son was in the hallway, his hair dripping wet, a towel wrapped around his waist. He looked at me sheepishly.

I reached out and gave him a hug.

Sept. 28, 2004

Adult friends give son a place in their world

At halftime during a recent Rickards High School football game, I left.

Not because the game wasn't exciting. (It was.) Not because I don't support the team. (I do.)

I left because it brought back too many memories of my own adolescence. Confusion. Fear. The feeling of being alone even while in a crowd.

Now that my son is a teenager, I get to live it all again. Lucky me.

I consider my adolescence a wasteland. I did a lot of things, went a lot of places, was around a lot of other teenagers. But what made it so barren was the lack of something essential — grown-ups.

Sure, my parents were around, but they weren't the ones who could help me escape the emotional claustrophobia that would suddenly envelop me.

What I yearned for was an adult to reach out and take an interest in me.

But there was no one. Maybe the reason was that I didn't have much of an extended family or that I moved from the Midwest to South Florida when I was 13. Whatever the reason, my personal landscape seemed devoid of adults.

I like to think that my oldest son has it better. Since he was born, his world has been peopled with grown-ups who are genuinely interested in him. They've taken him camping and out to dinner; they've helped him build gecko cages and catapults; they've encouraged him to garden; and they've exposed him to opera. One took him on his first driving lesson, and another had him over to watch the 1962 version of "The Manchurian Candidate." For years, whenever she'd breeze into town, one woman would call him up and suggest an adventure.

"David, want to go swim with the manatees?" she'd ask, and before I knew it, he'd be piling diving suits and flippers into the trunk and tying a canoe onto her car for a trip to Central Florida.

Then there's politics, his favorite subject. A slew of people are willing to listen to him ramble on about everything from President Bush to a new rule at his school. One recent night, the mother of one of his friends drove him home — but they were having such an interesting discussion that he didn't get out of the car until 20 minutes later.

His adult friends don't prevent him from going through normal adolescent stuff. I still see the look of insecurity in his eyes, his puzzlement at the ways of the world, his surprise when nothing turns out the way he imagined.

But with the help of caring adults — people besides Terry and me — I think he'll navigate these teenage years with a lot more confidence than I did.

And someday, when he's older, I hope he'll encourage teens to ramble on, or build a pet cage, or watch an old movie. Perhaps a lucky one will even get to swim with the manatees.

Oct. 12, 2004

Say a prayer as Israel buries its dead

When someone starts comparing Israel's policies to apartheid or criticizes the wall that it's erecting to keep Palestinians out, my blood begins to boil.

Terrorists are *blowing up* people on buses, at hotels, in restaurants and in markets. People read the morning paper to see whether they know anyone who died in the latest blast. Maybe the wall seems silly, but to those who've had to pick up a human head that has rolled into the gutter after a suicide bomb, at least it's something. Since it was built, the deaths have decreased. Don't you *get* it? This isn't about Israel trying to squish a tiny, helpless people. This is about safety.

But then when I hear a person talk about *those people*, how you can't trust Palestinians, how they all teach hate and violence, my temperature rises, too.

These people are exhausted. Many are unemployed. They are humiliated every day by umpteen searches. Their electricity and water are constantly being cut off, and some of their homes have been bulldozed to the ground. Many of their children have watched playmates shot dead right before their eyes. Don't you *get* it? This isn't about an intrinsically evil people. This is about justice.

My passion for both sides suddenly cools, however, after I read the statistics.

By mid-October, five Israelis had been killed in the latest conflict with Gaza — including two children, ages 2 and 4. One boy had his legs blown off.

Within weeks of the children's deaths, 115 Palestinians were killed in Israeli attempts at retaliation. *One hundred fifteen.* One of them was a 75-year-old woman, shot while breaking fast on the first day of Ramadan. Another was a 13-year-old who walked too close to an Israeli outpost. The soldiers thought she was carrying a bomb. Her backpack held nothing but books. Rhetoric now means nothing. The dead must be buried.

I think nothing will change until we can say to one another: *Your dead are my dead. My dead are yours.*

As an American Jew, I'll take one small step in that direction right now. I'll break with tradition and recite *kaddish*, a traditional Jewish mourning prayer, for the innocent civilians on *both* sides.

Surprisingly, the prayer isn't about death or sorrow or the afterlife. It starts by acknowledging God's greatness and ends with a prayer for peace. I trust God sees the larger picture, knows a way out of this mess. Because, frankly, here on earth we're stuck.

Dear God, teach us to do better by our dead.

Oct. 26, 2004

Gays were silent on election's hot topic

In 11 states, voters race to the polls because millions of children don't have health insurance! Because millions go to bed hungry! Because many can't read!

They're fed up, by golly, and this time they're going to vote for MORAL ISSUES!

Don't you wish.

Instead, a major issue on Election Day was gay marriage.

It's perplexing. Didn't people watch the presidential debates? John Kerry said he *opposed* gay marriage. John Edwards said he *opposed* gay marriage. Even Hillary Clinton, the liberal everyone loves to bash, said no, no, she *didn't* support gay marriage.

Not one political leader had the courage to stand up on this one.

Gays were left hanging out there in the breeze, by themselves. We were forced to vote for somebody who would deny us our civil rights. How many people do that?

Now, in the days following the election, we get to hear how gays just asked for too much, too soon.

I say we didn't ask for *enough*. We wimped out. With little show of outrage, we let people get away with saying that marriage should be between only a man and a woman.

We know better. Every day we live the reality that two women or two men can indeed be married. And those around us know it, too.

So why were we all so silent?

The biggest reason, of course, is that we didn't want George Bush to win.

But I think a friend of mine — who's straight — hit on another reason. She said the entire Democratic Party was gay-baited. Guilt by association. Everyone freaked and retreated.

But mimicking the Republican Party on the gay issue didn't work. People voted for Bush anyway.

Let's not retreat anymore. Let's be bold. Let's hold our elected officials accountable. No more of this mealy-mouthed "Some of my best friends are gay" stuff while opposing our civil rights.

Next election, let's get people to rush to the polls for *real* moral issues — poverty, hunger, health care, education. And let people who love each other live their lives.

Nov. 9, 2004

Respect for Mom grows as years pass

Shortly after I had led folks in a rousing rendition of "Lots of Latkes" at a recent Hanukkah party, my 15-year-old son took me aside and let me know just how *embarrassed* he was. I'd been *too* enthusiastic. I was *forcing* it on people. Didn't I know when to stop?

He talked so loudly, he couldn't hear my heart breaking.

But after the initial jolt of pain, I remembered a similar incident in my own youth. One day when I was in the kitchen, my older sister looked at me and said, "You're just like Mom!"

I was horrified. *I* was like *her?* I didn't say anything, but my mother, who was standing nearby, saw the look on my face. She said something like, "Now, *that* would be the worst thing in the world."

At the time, I thought it was. I felt we were as different as night and day — and I wanted it that way. We were already on the opposite sides of issues from abortion to vegetarianism. I wasn't going to be like her.

That sentiment continued through most of my 20s, particularly as our lifestyles seemed to grow further and further apart. Even today, we stay away from certain subjects. Before the presidential election, we talked about the candidates for less than five minutes before our blood started to boil.

But somewhere between my teenage years and now, sometime after I had a child, other feelings about my mother began to take root. Respect. Admiration. Pride.

My mother was, and continues to be, the moral center of our family. While we disagree on social issues, she's right on target with all the larger values — love, kindness, forgiveness, honesty. She told me that the world was pretty much divided into "givers" and "takers," and that I should strive to be a "giver." She couldn't stand people who talked only about themselves, and she encouraged me to listen to others. She taught me to appreciate the beauty of everything, from a single hibiscus blossom to a spectacular South Florida sunset. Material things mattered little to her; she always went straight for the heart.

It took me a long time to understand that many people didn't have this kind of moral compass in their families. For me, it was always there, guiding me even during the years when I was most estranged from her.

Today I try to emulate her. I like to think that some of her light is rubbing off on my kids. If someone were to say I was just like her, I'd be proud.

My son may never feel that way. But when he's older and he hears a strain of "Lots of Latkes," I hope he can remember his foolish old mother and smile.

Dec. 4, 2004

Sabbath Outing

Noah and I are ready for the creek walk. He has a net in one hand and a clear plastic container with a handle in the other. I'm toting a white garbage bag he insisted I take so we can pick up trash. I have a small notebook in my pocket, and we're both wearing water shoes.

It's Shabbat, the day of rest, a time to leave work behind and tune in to what's important. But my mind is racing. As we step down into the creek at Koucky Park in Indian-head Acres, I decide to let go, to focus on what's in front of me: the limestone creek bottom, the ankle-deep water gurgling past me, the damsel fly with black wings and iridescent-green body landing on a nearby elephant ear.

Eight-year-old Noah is already scooping the water with his net, trying to catch minnows — mosquito fish, to be exact. It's one of the few kinds of fish that live in this water. He hops over the rocks, skirting a waist-deep pool of water with ease. He's been visiting this creek since he was a toddler.

I wish I had known a similar patch of earth as a child. Even one tiny piece. A chunk of land I had dug my toes in, rolled around in, smelled deeply; where I had listened to the wind rush through the trees, tasted its rain water, cupped its bugs in my hand. A place that would pull me back, even years later, whispering, "You belong here."

But I have no such place.

I'm among the many rootless Americans who have a tenuous tie to the land. In the Chicago suburb where I grew up, I saw little wildlife. Trees — certainly good climb-ing trees — were scarce. I never got near a natural body of water. After moving to Florida when I was 13, I never returned.

Fort Lauderdale wasn't much better. In 1970, it was booming — new developments popping up everywhere, land razed and carved up. A true paved paradise.

Then 27 years ago year ago I came to Tallahassee, rumbling in on a Greyhound bus late at night, and caught my first glimpse of the live oak trees along Park Avenue. In the dim light of the streetlamps, I could see the outline of their thick girth and the dark sprawling branches with clumps of Spanish moss hanging down and swaying in the breeze. I couldn't see them, but I knew their roots went on forever. I wanted to call this place home.

But it's not that easy. Knowing a place in a deep, in-your-guts way takes time. I've claimed this land, but I'm not sure yet that it's claimed me.

*****

I reach down and pick up the tiny notebook that has fallen out of my pocket into the creek. I dab the pages with tissue, irritated that the ink has started to run.

"Sorry, Mom," Noah says, putting his arm around my waist. It's not his fault. I shrug and let out a long sigh. That's when I hear the "Plop!"

Noah looks up at me, his eyes shining, and then rushes over to the bank where the sound came from. He plunges his net into the water and brings up his prize — a large bullfrog and a tiny crayfish.

"We bingoed!" he cried.

If my notebook hadn't fallen out and we hadn't stopped, we would have missed it. My irritation gives way to gratitude.

The bullfrog isn't that unusual, but the crayfish is. Although this creek looks sweet, it doesn't support many small organisms — about six at tops: crayfish, mosquito fish, snails, damsel fly larvae, midges and worms. That's because it's not really a creek, at least not any more. It's a ditch. Other "real" creeks in the area support upwards of thirty-five species of animal life.

This creek was once one of those, originating near the present-day electric substation on Chowkeebin Nene, one of Indianhead's major north-south roads. Water would seep out of the ground near there and start flowing south through the floodplain that edges Optimist Park. When the heavy rains came, the water would overflow the banks, creating a swamp until the water slowly sank into the ground. At one time the creek was dammed up just north of Hokolin Nene, forming a lake. People used to canoe and sail boats in the water.

Then that all changed. After a heavy storm in the late 1950s, the dam broke and was never repaired. Today the original creek is almost dried up, and 30 feet east of its remnants runs a huge ditch dug by the City of Tallahassee. Rainwater could now gush into the ditch and be quickly transported south. During big storms, Noah and my older son, David, beg me to let them go down to the creek. They love seeing the water, which is usually about ankle-deep, turn a coffee-and-cream color and rise to over 10 feet, swirling and swooshing under the street culvert, racing downstream.

The ditch solved the flood and mosquito problem, but the creek paid the price. The gushing water scoured out the habitats of many organisms, allowing only a few sturdy ones to survive. The water also eroded the ditch's bank, causing some parts of the ditch to now be 10 feet wide. The real creek — which you can still find along the greenway trail behind Optimist Park — is stagnant.

You can't change the natural flow of things without consequences. Don't I know. As I stood looking at the crayfish that Noah promptly put into his plastic container, I was grateful that at least this small animal had survived. I've changed the natural flow of things more than once in my life, and I pray that, despite the disruption, not everything is destroyed.

I was raised Catholic but totally rejected the religion as an adult. I felt it was too patriarchal, too rigid, so I threw it out in one fell swoop when I was barely 18. Later, in my 30s, I forged a whole new path by converting to Judaism. This religion seemed more open and expansive. It welcomed intellectual rigor, yet had deep roots and a rich history. This was a place for me.

But again, it's not that simple. As the years go on, I grow to love Judaism more, but I also mourn what I let go. Nothing in my Jewish life resonates with my youth. When I light Shabbat candles, put on my *tallit* (prayer shawl) or recite prayers in Hebrew, nothing feels familiar. The Jewish melodies, even though I may like them, don't awaken old childhood memories, tying me to past generations. I'm like the new ditch that replaced the creek — more water runs through it, but I'm scoured clean of my former life.

I like to think that new life is coming back to my spiritual river. But I want to do better than the Indianhead ditch. Six species aren't enough for me — I want all 35.

*****

The garbage bag is getting heavy. We've barely gone a few hundred yards down the creek, and we've already collected so much trash the bag is ripping.

"Look at this!" Noah yells, pointing to a half-submerged basketball. He pulls and yanks and digs around it until he finally lifts it out of the creek bottom. After emptying it of water and sand, he puts it in with the other garbage: soda cans; beer bottles; a strip of garden hose; a red, white and blue flannel shirt; white and brown plastic bags; broken glass. We decide to leave the bag on the side of the bank and retrieve it on our way back.

Garbage isn't the only thing "unnatural" around here. So is a lot of the vegetation. Among the native hickory, black cherry, pine and oak trees, you have the mimosa tree, which sprouts pink powder-puff balls in the spring. It's from Australia. Covering a lot of the ground, particularly near Optimist Park, is wandering jew, a green-leafed plant with small white flowers blooming from spring through fall. It's from South America. In this country, it's considered invasive, taking over the forest floors and not allowing native species to grow. Then there's Chinese tallow and skunk vine from Asia, kudzu from Japan and air potato plants from Africa and Southeast Asia.

The vegetation is all mixed up, a jumble of native and nonnative, so much so that the average person doesn't know the difference. We may long for the pristine, for the authentic, but we have a hard time finding it in the natural world. The same can be said of our own bodies and souls. Sometimes it feels like we're a mix of fragments, each pushing and pulling against one another, competing for ground space. It's hard to figure out which ones really belong here.

That's why every morning I recite the Jewish blessing: *Elohai neshama she-natata be tehorah hi.* Oh God, the soul you have placed within me is pure.

There is a piece of me, beyond the Catholic or the Jew, the native or nonnative, that is pure in its essence. Most of the time I can't feel it. Most of the time I don't even know it's there. But for a few short moments in the morning, wrapped in my *tallit*, I affirm this purity in myself.

Walking in the creek, I suddenly stop. Noah is way ahead of me now, trying to catch minnows again. I close my eyes, tilt my face toward the sky and feel the sun's warmth pour over my cheeks. When I open my eyes, there's a cardinal perched on a nearby branch. Its feathers are stunning, bright red, pure.

*****

"Mom! Come here!" Noah yells from the large concrete culvert that runs beneath Hokolin Nene. I'm down below, at the edge of the embankment, which has been covered in cement to prevent erosion.

I shake my head *no*, and sit down on the huge tree limb that's running parallel to the ground.

"Oh, come on, Mom!" he yells again. "Please?"

Now I understand. He wants to go through the culvert to the other side. I stand up and climb my way up to him.

He grabs my hand and starts pulling me through the tunnel, baby step by baby step. I'm slightly bent over, looking down at the water, which is getting black and blacker as we get farther away from the culvert opening.

"Are you scared?" I ask Noah.

"I can't see the bottom," he says. "What if there's snakes in here?" But he continues on, holding fast to my hand. As the light from the other side of the tunnel gets brighter, his grip lessens.

"I can see the bottom now," he exclaims, then lets my hand go.

Going into dark, unknown places. Who wants to do that? But if someone's with you, it's not so bad.

I think of the Hebrews, wandering in the wilderness for 40 years. Which way should they go? This way? That? They had to rely on a cloud by day and pillar of fire by night.

Then one day, the sky darkened, lightning flashed, and God spoke from the quaking mountain. It was so awesome, no one person could withstand it.

But they weren't alone. They had each other. Being together allowed them to listen to the Voice.

Going back through the culvert, Noah doesn't hold my hand. He practically gallops through, his fear of snakes suddenly gone. Looking down the long tunnel, I see his silhouette when he reaches the other side. He never even looks back.

*****

It takes us two hours to explore about a block's worth of creek. That's Sabbath time for you. Elongated and unrushed. My racing mind has finally settled down.

On our way back, Noah sees a zebra longwing. Governor Lawton Chiles designated the longwing as the state butterfly in 1996. The black butterfly with yellow stripes roosts in flocks and sleeps so soundly you can pick it off the roost and return it later without waking up any of its family members. Every night it returns to the same perch. During the day, it flies slowly and doesn't startle easily. A Sabbath butterfly.

But the one Noah found isn't just slow. It's dead. He picks it up and asks me to carry it home. Farther down the stream, I also pick up the brimming garbage bag that we had placed on the bank earlier. In a few minutes, we will climb up the embankment near Chocksacka Nene and walk a few houses down to our home.

But before we get there, a huge bird suddenly swoops down near the water, and then flies up to a low branch in a tree. Another one follows. Noah stops dead in his tracks and motions me over. We're not more than 30 feet away. I can't believe my eyes — two red-shouldered hawks. In my 27 years in this area, I've never seen even one so close.

We hold our breath, not wanting to scare them away. We stare. One of them, which had its back turned to us, suddenly turns around and looks down at us. We get a full view of its russet-colored chest.

"It's like he wants us to get a good look," Noah whispers. I nod in agreement. The birds take off again, swooping down and then up to another branch. They continue this way, flying and perching, flying and perching, until they finally take off over the trees and out of sight.

My heart is pounding. I look down at Noah, and he wraps his arms around my waist. We stand this way for several minutes, feet in the ditch's water, surrounded by garbage and invasive plants. But part of us is also up there, flying high beneath the hawk's wing, listening to a voice that says "Welcome home, o soul."

Punched by cancer, picked up by love

The day of the tsunami, I found a lump in my left breast. As I watched the news accounts of a wall of water slamming into the shore half a world away, a tidal wave of fear arose inside me.

It would be several weeks before my suspicions were confirmed. But even before I heard the words "invasive ductal carcinoma," I identified with the tsunami victims. One minute you're fine and then — boom! — everything has changed.

Some people have told me it doesn't seem fair that a fairly young woman, the mother of three, should get this dreaded disease. But I think: Why not?

This past year, I followed two boys with Duchenne muscular dystrophy, and then wrote about their lives. They're both in wheelchairs and need assistance for many daily tasks. Their future is uncertain.

Definitely not fair.

In August, a 24-year-old woman I know who had just moved to California to seek fame and fortune was diagnosed with brain cancer. What's fair about that?

And then, of course, there are the tsunami victims — babies, elders, moms and dads, all swept away in a matter of moments.

The suffering of others doesn't lessen my own. It's still there. Sometimes I wake up in the middle of the night when the kids are asleep and think: *What if I weren't here? In the morning everyone would get up, go about daily life, carry on without me. Soon my almost 3-year-old would forget my face.* As I lie there in the darkness, sorrow corkscrews through my chest, leaving me gasping.

But having kindred spirits helps tremendously. I feel fortunate that I have the examples of Aaron and Josh, the boys with Duchenne's, and Katie, the young woman with brain cancer. I have followed their lives closely this past year, wondering how they could manage to live with so much spirit in the face of such uncertainty.

The answer, I learned, is simple: one step at a time. They're my role models now as I recover from a mastectomy, travel back and forth from Tampa to participate in a clinical trial, deal with chemotherapy, lose my hair and sweat my survival statistics.

The reality is that no one is safe from tidal waves. There's one out there waiting for each of us. One day it will hit.

The good news is that, just as they did for the tsunami victims, people come out of the woodwork to help. I can't count the acts of kindness that have come my way in the past several months.

Suffering may be part of the human condition, but so is love.

April 5, 2005

A bead up a 3-year-old's nose? 'Dora did it!'

My son David banged on the bedroom door, waking me from an afternoon nap.

"Jenna stuck a bead up her nose!" he exclaimed. "Come downstairs!"

By the time I stumbled into Jenna's bedroom, Terry had unwound a paper clip, gently slid it up our 3-year-old's right nostril and pulled out a blue bead.

"Did you put any more up there?" Terry asked.

Jenna nodded solemnly. "Five," she said, holding out all her fingers. We immediately aimed a light up her nose again, even though we knew she was exaggerating the numbers. Terry swore she sighted a pink one.

"Don't *ever* put anything up your nose," I admonished her, dreading the thought of a deep nasal excavation. Seeing my concern, she blurted out, "Dora did it!"

Her Dora the Explorer doll had been one naughty girl of late. That ripped-out page in the Winnie the Pooh book? Dora did it. Those crayon marks on her bedroom wall? Yep, Dora's fault. The brown-haired wonder also hits Jenna, says bad words and won't "co-OP-erate."

Now the bead up the nose.

Well, however horrifying Dora's offense might be, it's pretty classic. According to Dr. Javier Escobar, medical director of the Bixler Emergency Center at Tallahassee Memorial Hospital, at least two kids a week come to the emergency room with things jammed in their nostrils. In one case, the parent had brought the child in because of a foul smell. Turns out the kid had shoved a piece of jelly candy up his nose. When it was pulled out, it already had fuzzy green mold on it.

But the one that really takes the cake was mentioned in a column by my former colleague Keith Thomas, whose daughter stuck a Lego up her nose more than a decade ago. The emergency-room medical director told him that the strangest item *he'd* ever pulled out was a musical device found in a greeting card.

"Whenever you pressed the nose," the doctor said, "it played a musical tune."

Like Keith's daughter, my son Noah also stuck a Lego up his nose. Two, actually. The first one came out easily; the second one was more stubborn.

"Noah! Noah! Do this!" David shouted, blowing his nose as hard as he could. Noah tried it. Immediately, we heard "clink-clink-clink" as the Lego scudded across the bathroom floor.

That trick didn't work with Jenna. Not sure whether another bead was up there, Terry took her to the walk-in clinic. After checking her nose with a lighted instrument, then blowing air into her mouth through a mask and alternately holding each nostril closed, the doctor was pretty sure nothing was up there.

We breathed a sigh of relief.

Escobar said if you discover something up your child's nose, stay calm. Check to see whether you can easily remove the object. If you can't, don't fiddle with it because you risk getting it stuck even worse. Take your child to the doctor, who will have special forceps to remove the object. Occasionally, a child may have to be put under for a few seconds.

The best advice, of course, is to prevent it from happening in the first place. Keep tiny objects out of the reach of young children. Tell your kids never to put anything in their nose. And if you have a Dora in the house, lock her up — you never know what she might do next.

Aug. 16, 2005

Pardon me while I slow down for cancer

Parade magazine, in announcing its story on Olivia Newton-John, recently wrote on the cover: *"This four-time Grammy-winner didn't let breast cancer slow her down. Not for a second."*

Not for a *second*.

Right.

Somehow I don't think that's what Newton-John said. "Breast cancer? It was a cinch."

Me? I missed a second. Or two. Or a few hundred thousand.

But this kind of cancer mythology runs pretty rampant. It reminds me of my pregnancy days. Women who didn't show much were talked of in awed tones. "You can barely tell she's pregnant!" people would gush.

My thought: And this is some kind of virtue?

Now I'm hearing similar comments about cancer survivors. "She didn't miss *a day* of work!" "He played tennis *every day* he was on chemo!" "You'd never know she was in treatment!"

Those of us who missed weeks of work and had days we could barely crawl out of bed hear these remarks and think: "I must be a wimp."

I do. Or at least I used to. Something snapped when I read the *Parade* headline.

The fact is that cancer often slows you down, tosses you about, pummels your weary body until you're a mass of quivering flesh. So why pretend that a survivor doesn't miss a beat?

I think it's fear — of losing control, of being vulnerable. If people can convince themselves that it's just something we take in stride, then we keep that fear at bay.

I think it's the same reason people push "positive thinking" and a "good attitude." If I've heard it once, I've heard it a hundred times: A positive attitude will benefit my prognosis.

I don't quite buy it. Yes, a good attitude will improve my relationship with other people, help me get out the door in the morning on days I might otherwise mope around, push me to make the best of things. But somehow I don't think it'll make much difference in whether the cancer comes back. Think of the anguish of someone who has a recurrence thinking, "I must not have been *positive* enough."

I say a bad attitude can be healthy. It can take you places you otherwise might not go. For months before I was diagnosed, I had a dream that I opened a door in my house and discovered several rooms I had never known were there.

Those who interpret dreams say that houses often represent the dreamers themselves. I think that's true for this dream. Cancer opened up whole new places inside of me.

But if I always push away the thought of death, refuse to consider that cancer might do me in, I'll never step through that doorway. It's only my bad attitude that will force me. I want to know what's inside.

So it's OK that my life has slowed down, that negativity overtakes me now and then. I might not become the poster child for breast cancer, but at least I won't have to pretend.

Sept. 20, 2005

The sweet, the sad on Port St. Joe beach

I often read books or watch dark, artsy movies trying to glean some truth about life. The truth I've found most recently came from a kids' movie, based on the children's book "Because of Winn-Dixie."

In the story, 10-year-old India Opal Buloni moves to Florida. She has a hard time fitting in, but befriends the librarian, Miss Franny.

One day Miss Franny tells her about her great-grandfather, Littmus W. Block, who at 14 lied about his age and enlisted to fight in the Civil War. He thought he'd be a hero. Instead, he learned that war was hell — and lost his mother, father and three sisters.

The world was "a sorry affair" that needed more sweetness, he concluded. So later in life he started a candy factory and made Littmus Lozenges.

That was long ago. The factory had long since closed down. But Miss Franny happened to have Littmus Lozenges in her desk drawer.

Opal popped one into her mouth. It tasted like root beer and strawberry, but it also made her sad.

"There's a secret ingredient in there," Miss Franny said.

"I know," Opal said. "I can taste it. What is it?"

"Sorrow," Miss Franny said. "Not everybody can taste it. Children, especially, seem to have a hard time knowing it's there."

"I taste it," Opal said.

"Well, then," Miss Franny said, "you've probably had your share of sadness."

And she had. Opal's mother had left her and her father when Opal was 3.

At night, Opal lay in bed pondering it all. She thought "how life was like a Littmus Lozenge, how the sweet and the sad were all mixed up together."

Bingo.

Sometimes life is described as an alternating series of ups and downs. In truth, though, we often experience those ups and downs *in the same moment.*

I had a small taste of simultaneous ups and downs over the weekend. I was camping at Port St. Joe with family and friends, something we've done every October for almost a decade. My 3-year-old was ecstatic, racing up and down the beach, throwing her body onto the sand to feel the waves rush over her and later skipping along the beach in the moonlight. My 16-year-old, on the other hand, was bored. He never even went into the water and spent an afternoon asleep in the tent. The magic he'd experienced in his younger days was gone.

Meanwhile, I wore a T-shirt constantly to keep the sun off my chest because I was in the middle of radiation treatments. Watching my kids, I grew wistful, wondering whether I'd be around for many more of these October trips.

But I was also wildly happy, kayaking among jumping fish, watching a pair of mating horseshoe crabs glide past my boat like ice skaters in perfect unison.

The weather was fantastic — hot enough to swim, cool enough to be comfortable. The mosquitoes, however, were ferocious.

Was it a good trip? Was it bad?

Neither. Both.
It was a Littmus Lozenge weekend.

Oct. 25, 2005

What must we protect? Innocence, beauty

Last week as Jenna and I walked hand in hand to her preschool, she informed me she wasn't scared of the monsters in her room anymore because I would "protect" her.

Surprised that my 3-year-old used such a word, I asked, "What do you mean, I'll 'protect' you?"

"You'll keep me safe," she replied matter-of-factly. Then she looked up at me with such innocent confidence, my throat grew tight.

That word "protect" came up again a few days later when I attended a fundraiser at Wakulla Springs State Park sponsored by the Friends of Wakulla. At twilight, vocalist Velma Frye stood on a platform in front of the springs, flocks of ibis passing overhead, and sang sweet and cool and clear as the river.

I will never forget you. I will always protect you.
I will never forget you. I will always protect you.

My throat grew tight again. For 30 years I have visited these springs — sometimes during summer with its shouts of laughter and chilling waters, sometimes during winter with its stillness and its fires crackling inside the lodge.

The springs have always filled me up.

But during this time, the springs have declined. Many days, instead of clear blue-green, the waters run dark. The glass-bottom boats don't even attempt to go out.

Hydrilla, an invasive nonnative plant, grows rampant. It snuffs out the natural eelgrass. The brown spiral shells of apple snails, once so bountiful, are gone. Their disappearance has caused the brown-and-white-flecked limpkins that fed on the snails to flee, their plaintive cry a distant memory.

Kur-r-ee-ow, kow, kow, kow, kr-ow, krow.

Oh, come back, come back, I pleaded silently, as the light faded and the song ended. *I will never forget you.*

But can I protect you?

The Friends of Wakulla (www.wakullasprings.org) and others are trying to do just that. Members raise money, collect data and lobby government officials, all in the hopes of stemming the tide of decline.

Perhaps it makes a difference. Perhaps not.

No matter how much I want to keep the monsters at bay, some will eventually come crashing into my daughter's life. So, too, the springs will likely be in jeopardy, time and time again.

But I will never stop trying to keep my daughter safe. Wakulla Springs, the watery soul of the Big Bend, deserves the same commitment.

Nov. 15, 2005

'Holy Night' sparkled beneath the stars

When Sandy Fulton recently petitioned the Leon County School Board to *mandate* Christian music during school concerts, my first thought was: Has this woman ever been forced to sing a song opposed to her beliefs?

It's one thing to sing a Hanukkah song about a dreidel or the lighting of candles, quite another to sing about a "savior" you don't believe in.

I have a unique perspective on this. I grew up Catholic, but as an adult I converted to Judaism. When I was younger, I never thought twice about singing Christmas carols in any crowd. But once I had kids and converted, those savior-themed songs stuck in my throat.

My older son feels the same way. He once complained about having to sing a Christian song at his otherwise politically correct school.

Just last week my younger son, Noah, sang in the elementary all-state chorus in Tampa. Four of the eight songs were religious. And not just mildly so. We're talking "Benedictus and Hosanna." For weeks he belted out those songs around our house, working on the high notes. While most were based on psalms or Old Testament stories, the Latin words or gospel feel to the melodies gave them a distinct Christian feel.

My preference is that school and all-state choirs choose more neutral songs. There have to be a zillion choices out there, for Pete's sake.

But, as with so much in life, boundaries are seldom clear-cut.

On Christmas Eve, Terry and I were walking around our neighborhood with Noah and our 3-year-old daughter, Jenna, looking at all the Christmas lights. The night was dark and chilly. The lights shone brightly over the yards. As I held Jenna's hand, I suddenly began singing every nonreligious carol I knew: "Rudolph the Red-Nosed Reindeer," "Santa Claus is Coming to Town," "We Wish You a Merry Christmas," the works.

Then we grew quiet. My cheeks were cold. The stars twinkled. Suddenly, a song bubbled up inside, my favorite Christmas carol of all time: "O Holy Night."

In particular, I've always loved this line: "A thrill of hope, the weary world rejoices." As I sang it rounding a corner in Indian Head Acres, a shiver ran up my spine.

Whether you believe in Jesus as a savior or not, we all can relate to the words. Hope is a human yearning.

Perhaps singing words you can't really own is beneficial. A universal chord may be struck that wouldn't happen any other way.

On this one night, at least, singing them made this weary woman rejoice.

Jan. 17, 2006

Bald head isn't a sign of bravery

The first time my 3-year-old daughter's friend saw me bald, her jaw dropped and she blurted out, "Jenna's mommy's got a *head*!"

That was one of the lighter moments I experienced last year after my hair fell out in clumps because I was on chemotherapy. I shaved my head soon after I found long strands of hair in my nightly bowl of popcorn.

Then I was immediately faced with the whole "to bare or not to bare" decision. My choices ran the gamut.

When I was diagnosed with cancer, I swore I'd never wear those big old hats. I thought it would be like a neon sign announcing, "Cancer victim over here!"

So even before my hair fell out, I bought a wig. But being an ex-hippie, no-makeup kind of gal, I was too self-conscious to wear it, afraid it would look fake.

I wore turbans and baseball caps instead. They, of course, made me look just as conspicuous. One day when I was buying birthday party supplies for my daughter, the man behind the counter looked at me intently and said, "I just want you to know — you're beautiful."

Once when I was taking a walk, a guy in a pickup truck gave me the thumbs up, saying he knew someone who was going through the same thing. Other strangers in stores and restaurants would just look at me and ask, "Are you on chemotherapy?"

These comments never bothered me. Cancer is so prevalent, many people relate to it. It's just that when people would say things, I'd remember that I looked pretty odd. Besides being bald, I didn't have any eyebrows. I didn't even have any eyelashes. I felt I had an otherworldly, fish-like look. *E.T., go home!*

When I went back to work, I wore hats — small ones. But eventually I tired of those and just went bare.

That's when I started getting the "You're so brave" comments. My thought: Not really. I know rock star Melissa Etheridge and Florida Chief Justice Barbara Pariente got a lot of kudos when they appeared bald in public — and I applauded them, too. It was a thrill to see them bare it all. But I think those decisions are a matter of personality, not bravery. Some women are more "out there," some are more reticent. Women who wear wigs, scarves and hats can be just as courageous as the baldies.

Today my eyelashes and eyebrows are back and I have about an inch of hair on my head. Three weeks ago, as I sat in a beauty shop getting my first haircut in almost a year, I marveled at the wisps of hair gathering around the chair below me.

I hope I'll never be bald again. But if I have to make another decision about how much of my head to display, bravery will have nothing to do with it.

Feb. 7, 2006

Finding Isaac
and a lot more

My 3-year-old daughter came home one recent evening, threw her body across the couch and sobbed.

"Isaac is lost!" Jenna wailed.

Uh-oh. Isaac is a doll she got for Christmas. The moment she unwrapped him, it was love at first sight. Despite his pink pajamas and cap, she insists he's a boy, and she doesn't go anywhere without him.

Not even Jazzercise. That evening Terry had taken Jenna and Isaac to the exercise class at East Hill Baptist Church. Terry remembered that Jenna had carried him toward the car afterward, but somehow he hadn't made it home.

"Will you go find him?" Jenna sniffled, looking up at me plaintively.

The night was cold. I was exhausted. Getting into the car and driving back across town was the last thing I wanted to do.

But then a Patty Griffin song started rattling around in my head:

When you break down, I'll drive out and find you
When you forget my love, I'll try to remind you
And stay by you, when it don't come easy.

I remember when I was broken down in my mid-20s and Terry found me, her presence a balm for my melancholy soul. Ten years later, something inside me still wasn't completely healed. This time God found me and reminded me that love was part of the DNA of the universe.

All of us need to be found, to be reminded of love no matter what.

So after glancing back at Jenna's teary face, I sighed, put on my coat and got into the car. Maybe I'd find Isaac, maybe I wouldn't. But I had to try.

As I drove into the parking lot near the back of the church, I anxiously looked on the ground. I immediately spotted Isaac face down in the grass.

Before walking through the door at home, I hid Isaac in my coat. When I came in, I tried to look a little sad.

"Well, I looked and looked for him. . . ," I said.

Jenna's eyes widened, a fresh new set of tears about to start.

"I found him!" I exclaimed, pulling him out from under my coat with a flourish.

Jenna didn't say anything. She just reached out and pulled him close to her, looking intently into his eyes and rubbing the top of his head.

There was no need for words. Isaac was home.

Feb. 28, 2006

Picture this: A love story, 10 years later

I recently saw "Brokeback Mountain" and was swept up in the poignant parting scenes, the crashing, passionate reunions all under the Big Sky.

But I also felt like putting my hand on my hip and tapping my foot in impatience.

The movie was just another love story. And I've seen zillions of them.

What I'd like to see is this couple — or any other Hollywood movie couple — living together day in and day out for, say, I don't know, six months? Two years? Ten years?

We rarely get a glimpse of this part of a relationship on-screen.

"Well," you might say, "that's because it's mundane. It's boring."

But is it?

Anybody who has been in a good, long-term relationship knows that the really good stuff often doesn't happen for years, even decades. By then one facade after another has crashed to the ground, leaving you naked and vulnerable and often very cranky.

But it produces a rich, loamy soil, just the way table scraps and dead leaves do in compost. Much good can grow from it.

Besides, these marriages can be fun.

A psychologist friend of mine once asked me what I thought most good marriages had in common. My suggestions: good sex, mutual respect, support for each other.

Nope, she said. It was laughter.

I was startled at first, but then it made sense. Think about it. We're not talking about friends getting together over a few beers, all relaxed and primed for a good time. We're talking about guffawing amid the piles of laundry, with a toothbrush in your mouth before bedtime, after the dog pees on your shoe and your 3-year-old has dropped your cellphone down the toilet.

If you can still laugh in those situations, it speaks volumes about your relationship.

Some TV series cover this kind of relationship territory. But for the most part, Hollywood stays away, opting instead to show us film after film of people *falling* in love. Why not give a little more footage to people *staying* in love?

It's bound to be a blockbuster.

April 4, 2006

When the gay issue hits home

In more than a year as the faith editor, I've encountered this phenomenon a number of times: the gay issue as litmus test.

I'll be talking with a pastor or a congregant who will casually interject something like, "Well, we don't believe in gay marriage or anything."

It's a shorthand way of defining the church's beliefs. The assumption is that if you know where the church stands on that issue, you can infer where it stands on others.

When someone makes such a statement, I try to keep a straight face (no pun intended). "Do they know?" I wonder.

I'm a married lesbian. Terry and I had our first ceremony — illegal but love-sanctioned — in 1986 at the Unitarian Universalist Church in Tallahassee. The second ceremony — this time legal, still love-sanctioned — was in Canada in 2004. It was officiated by our own Rabbi Jack Romberg, who flew to Toronto to help us tie the knot a second time.

I assume the people I'm interviewing are unaware of that — and I don't clue them in. Although I've been "out" in my columns for seven years, I figure that isn't the time or place to talk about my personal life.

But inside I take note. And what surprises me every time is how much I *like* the person I'm sitting across from. The religious folks I've encountered in my job are by far some of the nicest people I've ever met. They're not the rabid-right religious fanatics whom some in the gay community fear. They're just regular folks, trying to do the right thing.

So I'm even more puzzled by this gay-marriage issue. Most of the people behind the Florida Marriage Amendment that will be voted on next year are from the religious community — maybe even some of the folks I've interviewed.

I wonder whether they realize how mean-spirited this law could become.

On the surface, the amendment is bad enough. It reads: *Inasmuch as marriage is the legal union of only one man and one woman as husband and wife, no other legal union that is treated as marriage or the substantial equivalent thereof shall be valid or recognized.*

It's not meant, some proponents say, to abolish such benefits as health insurance for domestic partners. But it could.

A similar amendment, passed in Michigan in 2004, has done just that. By the end of this year, for example, the University of Michigan will be forced to stop providing same-sex domestic-partner benefits to its employees. (University administrators are trying to work around the law, however, because, as the associate vice president for human resources recently wrote, "health insurance is a benefit of vital importance to our faculty and staff.")

The amendment could have other unintended consequences. The American Civil Liberties Union of Florida stated in a report that the Florida amendment could also result in loss of benefits for unmarried heterosexual couples and their children.

Just the possibility that some family could lose benefits stops my heart cold. The *Tallahassee Democrat* has provided domestic-partner benefits for more than five years. It's been a lifesaver for Terry, me and our three kids, particularly because Terry is self-employed. If she and one of the kids were kicked off my plan, she'd have to pay more than $700 a month to get covered — and that wouldn't include dental costs.

We're probably not in danger of losing the benefits, whether the amendment passes in Florida or not, because Gannett is a private corporation. (Typically, it's public institutions that are targeted.) And the folks at FAMU, TCC and FSU wouldn't be affected either — because the state never offered domestic-partner benefits in the first place.

But folks in other parts of Florida — who are already getting benefits — could be affected, including public employees in Broward and Monroe counties and ones in Gainesville, Key West, Miami Beach and West Palm Beach. And, of course, it could prevent public employers from *adding* domestic benefits in the future.

I know how important good benefits are. When I was diagnosed with cancer two years ago, I was fortunate to be covered under one of the best insurance policies in the country. I believe the care I got saved my life. I shudder to think of Terry's getting cancer and having only bare-bones health insurance because she couldn't be on mine.

Maybe the religious folks I talk with don't understand the harm the amendment could cause. Or maybe it's not as important to them as their religious convictions.

In either case, when they take their stance against gay marriage, I feel as if I've been kicked in the gut.

July 21, 2008

Don't sit back and wait for change

About a week before the election, I ran into a friend of mine during a walk around the block. "Could it really happen?" we asked each other almost giddily. "Could Barack Obama really get elected?"

If he did, my friend reminded me, we would all have to do our part.

Our part.

Just days after the election, that's not what I hear people saying. Instead, it's "Let's see what he can do." Some say it with enthusiasm, hoping he'll have the golden touch to solve our problems. Others say it almost as a taunt, like they want him to run into roadblocks.

But these next four years will be not just a testing ground for Obama. They're a testing ground for us. That's what my friend meant by "our part."

Will we "reach across the aisle" from our own comfort zones to find common ground with those different from us? Will we be willing to be a maverick when needed? Will we sneer, call people names, complain, criticize and offer empty rhetoric instead of rolling up our sleeves and doing the hard work in the trenches?

Will we hold ourselves accountable — admit, for instance, that part of this economic crisis isn't just caused by the greed on Wall Street, but by our own desire for easy money and bigger houses? Instead of just expecting the government to solve this health-care mess, will we give up our bad eating habits, stop smoking and get more exercise?

Will we use our money wisely, be honest in our business dealings, stay morally consistent, address the hard questions, tell the truth?

What we expect of our politicians, we should expect of ourselves.

I know that I, for one, have my work cut out for me. That "reaching across the aisle" makes me squeamish. I like my comfort zone. And it's so much easier for me to complain than to change.

But this election offers me a challenge. Four years from now, will the world be better off than it is today?

When I go into the voting booth in 2012, not only will I ask that question of the candidates, I'll ask it of myself.

Nov. 9, 2008

In the park, with a child, God's blessing is revealed

By the end of last week, I was emotionally beat.

The anticipated layoffs at work were finally over, and although I still had a job, I continued to careen between tears, numbness, depression and anxiety.

By Sunday, my soul longed for a rest. Determined to do something positive, I pulled myself off the couch and went to Optimist Park with my 6-year-old daughter, Jenna.

It was the best decision I could have made.

The sun was so bright, the air so shining, just watching her slender body pedal her pink bike lifted my spirits. Instead of mulling things over in my mind, I looked upward to the top of the trees. Swaying pine needles. Red and yellow maple leaves. Pink camellia blossoms. Glossy magnolia leaves.

We lay down in the middle of the football field and looked up into the cloudless blue sky. Jenna picked up a tiny ground leaf and held it up above our heads, allowing the sun to shine through.

"Isn't that beautiful?" she gushed.

She snuggled in the crook of my armpit, and then got her face really close to mine. "I love you, Mom!" she whispered, her liquid hazel eyes about an inch from mine.

We heard a grasshopper snap nearby, and Jenna got on all fours and crawled up close to it. Just as she got near, it jumped away. Then we watched several bees buzzing and hovering close to the ground, barely distinguishable from the dried grass below them.

"I don't want one of them to sting me because then they'll die," she informed me solemnly.

We walked over to the large live oak tree on the edge of the park, our eyes running up and down the scaly bark of the trunk and the long branches that thrust out in all directions. We marveled at the carpet of acorns at our feet. Walking out from under the tree, Jenna said, "Come out here, Mom, and you can see how really big it is."

Walking back to the house with Jenna riding ahead of me, I realized I hadn't thought about money or jobs or what-are-we-going-to-do-in-this-recession for an entire hour and a half. The afternoon sun was slanting through the trees, shimmering off Jenna's body like a halo.

Holy daughter. Holy world.

With such blessings I can face my life again.

Dec. 13, 2008

Yearning leads us to God

When I was visiting recently with my 20-year-old son in Gainesville, he told me he didn't believe in God.

Religion was "magic." He was a cultural and social Jew, not a believing one.

My first thought was, "Where did I go wrong?" That was followed immediately by, "You were an atheist at that age, too."

When I told him this, he accused me of being smug. I, too, had detested religious folks who assumed I'd "come around" with age. Anyone who gave me the I-know-the-truth-and-you-don't attitude always turned me off.

But my son misinterpreted what I was saying.

I don't necessarily think some hard knocks and maturity will change him. I know many wise elders who have steered clear of God and religion their whole lives and don't have a lick of regret. He could very well grow up to be one of them.

No, what my son heard in my tone was my struggle to articulate why *I* had changed. I've never been very comfortable talking with my children about God, partly because I've had so many questions and doubts most of my adult life, and I needed time and space to work through them. I want them to have the same freedom.

So the best I could come up with was to tell my son that I felt God "existed" in the same way that love "existed" — even though you can't quantify, locate or research either one.

Just as some God-critics say that religion is only about fulfilling social and psychological needs, that it's more about trying to put a salve on life's hurts than a link to anything authentic, so one could also say that love is nothing more than the fear of being alone and the selfish needs for sex, money and possessions.

Critics also point to all the times that people have tortured, maimed and killed one another in the name of God. But people have killed their spouses — and even their children — in the name of love. Do these acts of violence negate God or love?

Bottom line is, we can't empirically prove either one's existence. Yet few people would say they don't "believe" in love.

That's because we don't love because of rationality. Love happens to us. It flows through us. Once we've experienced it, we know how it can move mountains.

Some of us — particularly intellectuals — don't allow God to "happen" in the same way. We don't want to be fools. We want our hard-core evidence.

My hope for my son is that he doesn't approach God or religion rationally. My faith started not with anybody witnessing to me or articulating a convincing argument.

It started with a yearning.

My advice to my son is: If you ever feel something similar, don't turn away, minimize it or argue it away. Pay attention. Be fearless. Let it lead you to its source.

Dec. 5, 2009

A moment of peace
emerges at a hospital

As I wait for my life partner to finish her medical procedure at Shands Hospital in Gainesville, I slide into a seat at the hospital's interfaith chapel.

Symbols from a dozen religions adorn the wall behind the altar. The room is empty. As I take a deep breath and close my eyes, I hear the clatter of dishes from the cafeteria across the hall, the click of heels along the corridor floor.

I've been reading "The Presence Process" by Michael Brown. Like Buddhists for hundreds of years and modern-day spiritual leaders such as Eckhart Tolle, author of the Oprah-endorsed "A New Earth," Brown emphasizes the importance of emptying our minds of both past events and concerns about the future in order to just be right here, right now.

He lays out an 11-week program that requires two 15-minute periods a day of meditation, combined with some reading material and a "Presence Activating Statement" each week. The first statement is: "I choose to experience this moment."

Most of us don't want to. In a place like Shands, an emotionally charged microcosm of the world, it's evident why. People here are sick, really sick. They come from all over the Southeast to get treatment from its two academic centers, three community hospitals and two specialty hospitals, including one for children.

All kinds of folks — one estimate is as high as 30,000 people a day — come through its doors. You can see toddlers, their arms in casts, being pulled in red wagons by parents; bald 10-year-olds walking the halls in hospital gowns; old folks hobbling along with walkers; skinny men clutching IV poles on wheels as they go outside for a breath of fresh air; interpreters using sign language to communicate with deaf patients; a granddad falling asleep in the waiting room while three grandchildren squirm in their chairs.

Some are hearing good news; others are bracing for the worst.

In the midst of all this swirling humanity are small points of pleasure — the smell of freshly ground coffee from the atrium cafe, the man in the Santa Claus hat playing carols on the piano, colorful tiles and mosaics that glitter and shine from an entire lobby wall, the child in the wagon smiling at a stranger.

In the chapel silence, my story blends with those in this massive medical complex. We all suffer, we all are blessed. We can, if we have the courage, embrace it all.

"I choose to experience this moment," I say softly.

I choose

This moment.

I choose

Just this.

In the silence that returns, I breathe at least one breath of peace.

Jan. 2, 2010

The kids (of lesbian moms) are all right

I hate it when people gloat — especially parents.

Not only is it irritating, but the reasons for the gloating can evaporate faster than wet footprints on a sunny Tallahassee sidewalk. No matter what your child has accomplished — or what you think you've done right as a parent — something will happen that lands you on your bum wondering, "Where did I go wrong?"

Still, I felt a little wave of smugness wash over me when I read about a recent study in *Pediatrics* magazine. It concluded that children of lesbians were not only as psychologically well-adjusted as those in straight families but, in some areas, even more confident and competent.

For years, studies have shown that children of gays and lesbians weren't much different from those in traditional families, but this is the first longitudinal study that followed children in lesbian households over a 17-year period. According to the *Pediatrics* article, children of lesbians scored higher in social, academic and overall competence and lower in social problems, rule-breaking and aggression than their counterparts in straight families.

The results surprised even the authors.

"It wasn't something I anticipated," said Nanette Gartrell in a *Time* magazine article.

The study results don't fit my kids to a T (lower rule-breaking? hmmm . . .), but I had to agree that all three display a healthy dose of self-esteem and competence — and so do the children in other lesbian households that I know.

When Terry and I started our family 21 years ago, we were confident — perhaps even a bit cocky — that we could raise our children as well as anybody else. But I would be lying if I didn't admit that, over the years, doubt has crept in.

Would my boys suffer from having two moms? Would my daughter relate well to the opposite sex? In the long run, would they feel deprived because they didn't have a male role model in the home?

The hammering from the critics didn't help. Everyone from the conservative right to President Barack Obama has insisted that any kid who doesn't have a dad is likely to face an array of problems, from dropping out of school to teen pregnancy.

Now we have a study that suggests two moms might have something to teach heterosexual parents.

But I'm not going to gloat over this. My initial smugness was only momentary. The older I get, the more I'm convinced that when men step up to the plate — whether it's to raise families, educate our children, help run religious institutions or tackle any number of other social endeavors — the better off all of us are.

One day I hope my sons will be among those men who are intensely involved in family and community life. And perhaps they'll participate not despite but because of their lesbian moms.

June 29, 2010

Village people salve more than cancer

It takes a village to get through cancer.

I've experienced this phenomenon twice now — when I got breast cancer five years ago, and then when my life partner, Terry, was diagnosed with non-Hodgkin's lymphoma in December.

The outpouring from friends and family, synagogue, neighborhood and workplace has been so profuse, we've been humbled. People have cooked us meals, taken care of our kids, given us counseling and hands-on healing, sent us cards and books, accompanied us to chemo treatments, listened to us as we cried and raged and slowly tried to get our lives back together.

We would often look at each other and ask, "How could we ever have gotten through this without all the help?"

We couldn't have.

Cancer gets people's attention. It's dramatic and life-threatening. And the bald head is sure to elicit sympathy.

Moreover, treatment often has a beginning and an end. While it's going on, people are willing to help out.

But as we were going through our crises, I often thought of the less dramatic but just as treacherous conditions people deal with — Alzheimer's disease, rheumatoid arthritis, back problems, depression. People struggle just to get out of bed. Pain is a daily companion.

I wonder whether these folks ever experience the village of help we did. I suspect not.

Perhaps their disease comes on slowly so no one is aware when things get really bad. Or friends and family don't know much about the illness and its devastating effects. People may hold back, not sure how to help.

But another obstacle may also be operating: People who are suffering may not allow themselves to receive help. They don't talk about their problems, hiding behind a veneer of "I'm fine, thank you." If someone offers assistance, they turn it down.

Perhaps they're too proud, too private or simply reluctant to be a burden. Whatever the case, the flow of village caretaking comes to a halt.

So I have two observations from the land of cancer: As a community, we need to support everyone who's in pain, no matter what the source. And when people reach out, those who are suffering need to let them.

A village operates best when it has both givers and receivers — and on any particular day, we can be on one side or the other.

Whichever one you're currently on, keep the flow going.

Aug. 1, 2010

Wonders come every day in ordinary ways

Terry called me on the phone one day, so excited she was almost breathless.

"The most beautiful bird is outside my office window!" she gushed.

Having been my life partner for many years, she knows I love birds. I wondered what unusual feathered friend was visiting today.

"What does it look like?" I asked immediately, trying to remember where I had last placed my "Peterson's Guide to North American Birds."

"It's blue with a white breast and a black ring around the neck and a pointy head!" she exclaimed.

"Terry," I said, suddenly amused, "that's a blue jay."

I should have added, a *common* blue jay. They're everywhere. Terry had just never *seen* one before.

We all do that — overlook the marvelous things around us. To truly see, we have to wake up.

I was reminded of this phenomenon when I saw the movie "Avatar." I got so engrossed in the world the producers had created — the glowing plants, the trees hanging in midair, the flying dragons — that I was almost homesick for it when I left the theater. I wanted to re-enter that world where everything was so alive and shining.

Then this summer, I spent four and a half days on a solitary, silent retreat in the Grassroots Community off Old St. Augustine Road. I didn't talk with anyone, watch TV or get on the computer. All I did was pray, meditate, do yoga — and eat, thanks to my kind hostess and friend Nechama, who would appear each day around 6 p.m. with a hot plate of food.

The best part was my series of walking meditations — slow, leisurely walks around the community. But just as in regular meditation, I didn't let my mind just flit from one thought to the next. I kept it focused on the here and now. Any time it drifted away, I brought it back to the present — the rustle in the trees, the cluster of pink blossoms dropping from a crape myrtle, the sweat dripping down my neck, the crunch of the stones underneath my feet.

One day I spent 45 minutes in a tiny piece of woods on Nechama's property. Normally I could have whipped along the trail in a matter of seconds. But that afternoon, I took my time.

The land was suddenly as rich and mysterious as anything I saw in "Avatar" — tiny white, almost translucent mushrooms popping up from the dark earth, the black and iridescent blue-green wings of the pipevine swallowtails, a zillion shades of green all around me. The cicadas would start their scratchy chorus, get louder, crescendo, then fade away. Just the sunlight illuminating a slice of tree bark almost brought me to my knees.

When you really see things for the first time, it's a holy moment.

Now I know I shouldn't have laughed at Terry that day. I should have agreed with her.

Blue jays are exquisite.

Sept. 12, 2010

Dates and prayer go a long way in a marriage

I hesitate to offer marriage advice. I'm not an expert, and my 27-year marriage isn't perfect.

But a few things have helped my relationship over the years, and I think they might be helpful to couples, both gay and straight.

So for what it's worth, I offer two recommendations: dates and prayer.

Couples, particularly those who have kids, should set up a weekly date day or night. It's similar to cleaning your house or maintaining your car. When you keep up with it, things run more smoothly.

Terry and I started going on a weekly date after our middle child was born. We had been together more than a decade by then, and we started none too soon.

Like most parents of young children, we had gotten caught up in the daily work of jobs, raising children, keeping up the house. The only time we even got to talk was late at night, when we were bushed. Funny — arguments tend to happen in those late-night hours, too.

Since our dates began, we laugh together more. We talk about other things besides the kids. We're more affectionate.

Not all our dates work out perfectly. We've spent a number of them hashing out a problem rather than having fun.

But more often, we have a great time. The baby sitter is worth every cent.

One caveat: Most dates should just be the two of you. If you spend them going to parties or out to the movies, you can hide from simmering problems. In one-on-one dates, unspoken tensions have a way of popping up quickly. That's part of the marriage maintenance.

My other suggestion is to pray for your partner.

I started this in the spring after I interviewed Frank Fincham, the eminent scholar and director of the Family Institute at FSU. Fincham's research found that people who specifically pray for the well-being of their mate are more prone to forgive that person than those who just think positively about their partner or just pray in general. Another study showed that praying specifically for a partner also reduces rates of infidelity. (For details, visit www.pss.sagepub.com and www.economist.com/node/16886238.)

At the time of the interview, stress was at an all-time high in my household.

"Don't a lot of people pray for their spouses?" I asked Fincham.

He asked me if I did, and I said I had recently prayed about a health issue with Terry. Fincham said praying about health was common — but what about praying just for the well-being of my partner?

It had never occurred to me.

He said that the prayer shouldn't be directed at how to change a partner — that would be disastrous. His suggestion was to pray for your spouse to have strength and direction during the day. Perhaps most important, pray that you become a blessing in your partner's life.

I started praying for Terry that very day.

The irritation I had felt toward her for months began to melt away. Instead of focusing on all the things that bothered me, I started seeing the preciousness of our relationship — and my responsibility to keep it sacred.

Dates and prayer may not be a cure-all for every marriage. But they're worth a try.

If nothing else, they're easier and cheaper than couples counseling.

Or divorce.

Oct. 17, 2010

Aunt Vicki brings the banquet

Most of us have a clear idea of what it means to be a good mother.

Nurturance, warmth, stability and self-sacrifice are qualities that come to mind. We frown on behavior that goes outside this box.

But what makes a great aunt?

Now, this is a role with latitude. Think of Auntie Mame, the freewheeling star of the 1958 film who introduced her nephew to people and concepts disapproved of by polite society. Her motto was "Life is a banquet, and most poor suckers are starving to death!"

Laura Ellingson and Patricia Sotirin, authors of "Aunting: Cultural Practices That Sustain Family and Community Life," write: "The aunt relationship is uniquely unburdened by normative expectations and role prescriptions. Even very 'bad' behavior may be deemed indicative of a 'good' aunt.

But wherever an aunt falls on the spectrum, the authors show how aunts, both biological and chosen, often provide the glue in families, offering a release valve for tensions, support for busy parents and a wider world view for children.

The book was the perfect gift for my children's Aunt Vicki, my closest friend for 30 years. In it, my 15-year-old son Noah inscribed: "You have always been the best and my most favorite aunt. I definitely wouldn't be the same person I am today without you."

Vicki Mariner has been around since Day One in each of their lives, helping Terry and me every step of the way. She's cradled their newborn bodies in her arms, attended birthday parties, bar mitzvahs, Shabbat dinners and graduations, and offered a quiet place of solace on five acres of land in Wakulla County that she shares with her husband, Jim.

Today she argues politics with my 21-year-old son, David, defending her Quaker pacifism against his more hawkish tendencies. She doesn't budge. Neither does he.

For years, she's taken Noah on camping trips to Colorado or to Quaker retreats in Central Florida. When Terry and I are pulling our hair out, convinced we won't survive his teen years, she reminds us, "He's such a great kid!"

But it is perhaps with our 8-year-old daughter, Jenna, that her aunting has blossomed the most. Every Thursday for most of Jenna's life, Vicki has appeared on our doorstep, dressed in warm shades of off-the-Goodwill-rack cotton clothes, a basket in hand filled with food she's already made — or will make — for our family.

She whirls in, taking note of the plants that aren't watered, the moldy food in the refrigerator, the curtains that need to be either opened or closed. She immediately sets about making things right.

She'll let the dogs curl up on Jenna's bed (something I forbid) and allow Jenna to take out every blanket and sheet to make a living-room fort. Although she'll tsk-tsk if she finds we've eaten at McDonald's, she'll make us extra-rich brownies with Ghirardelli chocolate.

But it's the time she spends with Jenna out at her place that I think Jenna will remember the most. Jenna knows the names of every one of Vicki's four goats, five chickens, two ducks and two cats. She races out to scoop out the eggs from the hen house and sits for hours in the goat pen, singing and watching the dwarf Nigerian goats, with their barrel chests and stubby legs, eat stacks of sweet gum leaves.

My favorite image: the two of them walking the goats around the sinkhole, the bells around the goats' necks tinkling as they walk, my long-limbed, curly-haired Jenna running to and fro, Vicki stopping to move a limb off the trail or usher the small herd over to a particularly tasty batch of leaves.

For the most part, my kids take Vicki for granted. She's always been there, coming and going, present at all the significant life events.

But as Noah is starting to note, he wouldn't be the same without her. Neither would the rest of us.

Life is a banquet — and Vicki makes sure that we're all getting a hearty meal.

Dec. 12, 2010

Do religious people make better neighbors?

Although one reason I joined organized religion in my 30s was to become a more compassionate person, I never considered it a prerequisite for being a giving person.

But statistically speaking, I was wrong.

Religious people, by pretty high margins, are better neighbors than their secular counterparts, whether you're looking at volunteering, practicing philanthropy, donating blood, helping someone find a job, getting involved with local politics or just spending time with someone who is blue.

Robert Putnam and David Campbell, authors of "American Grace: How Religion Divides and Unites Us," came to this conclusion after a review of the research, including their own survey, Faith Matters.

Here's some of what they found:

♦ Forty percent of worship-attending Americans volunteer regularly to help the poor and elderly, compared with 15 percent who never attend services.

♦ The most secular fifth of the population donates $1,000 a year to charitable organizations; the most religious fifth gives $3,000.

♦ The most religious fifth of the population belong to 34 percent more community organizations (such as Scouts and Red Cross) than the most secular fifth.

And people's religious beliefs or personal piety don't seem to affect their giving. What does matter is the number of religious friends they have.

The authors write: "In round numbers, people with many religiously based social connections are two or three times more likely to be civically engaged and generous, *even to purely secular causes*, than people with few such ties, regardless of how devout and observant they themselves are" (emphasis mine).

This may sound crass, but I think the faith community should use this as a marketing tool.

Increasing numbers of people consider themselves "nones," as in "no particular religion," particularly those born after 1980. Nones, who now represent 17 percent of the population, don't think organized religion has much to offer.

But however someone feels about preachers, God, church politics, the afterlife or the divinity of Jesus, these statistics suggest that the faith community is a breeding ground for generosity.

In an article published in *USA Today* in November, Putnam and Campbell wrote: "Not knowing exactly how religious friendships foster good neighborliness thus leaves open the possibility that the same sort of effect could be found in secular organizations. But they would probably have to resemble religious congregations — close-knit communities with shared morals and values. Currently, though, such groups are few and far between."

Right now organized religion offers the best option. Those who want to put their morals into action — or want their children to — might want to check it out.

Jan. 22, 2011

Retreats allow us to move toward God

Near the end of my time at Isabella Freedman Jewish Retreat Center in early July, a woman said her husband asked her how her "advance" was going.

In his mind, she wasn't retreating, she was advancing.

I loved it. In one word, he had summed up what retreats have been about for me the past 15 years. I've been on big group retreats, solo retreats, silent retreats and writing retreats. They've ranged from two to 10 days.

At some, I sang ecstatically, cried frequently and even found myself face down on the ground in thankfulness. At others, the silence settled over me like a warm blanket, causing the thoughts in my head to grow louder and louder until, one by one, I began to let them go.

But no matter how varied the retreat experience was, as I withdrew from my everyday routine, my parenting responsibilities, my TV and my cellphone, I took a leap toward God.

The formula is simple — slow down, keep distractions to a minimum and open the heart. God will show up.

Some may call it something else — insight, inner wisdom, deep knowing. But whatever one calls it, it's hard to discern in our hectic lives. God is with us every minute of the day, but just like a relationship with a spouse, there's a difference between going through the daily routines in each other's presence and really looking into one another's eyes.

What happens when you close the door and actually spend time alone? Intimacy grows exponentially.

When I went on my first retreat, I believed in God. Sort of. Maybe.

In reality, I was ambivalent.

Then I spent a week in the Catskills of New York, not once getting into a car. In the morning I went to prayer services, spent the day in classes and prayed again at night. I sang and danced and took long walks.

On Shabbat morning, we sang the morning blessings and a series of psalms. Then it was time for the *amidah*, the central Jewish prayer. Everything in the service leads up to this central moment, when we stand before God. At the Jewish Renewal retreat center I was attending, people often took this time to go off by themselves to recite the prayer before coming back to the group.

I walked to an open field and opened my arms to the sky. I didn't say a word. Soon I was doubled over, tears streaming down my face, a powerful presence sweeping through me.

It's hard to describe the inner workings of the soul. What turns it. How, exactly, it opens.

Let's just say that when I left that retreat, my ambivalence was gone.

I've never again had such an ecstatic moment. But the aftertaste of that morning in the field stays with me.

This last retreat in Connecticut was perhaps my most subdued. It was a small group of 30. We didn't pray together much and I didn't dance. I took a lot of naps.

But on Shabbat afternoon I sat on the dock by the lake, talking for almost two hours to one of the teachers. I poured out my heart to her, telling her about my spiritual struggles, my personal problems, what I felt God was calling me — no, pushing me — to do.

She listened with such splendid attention, I could feel myself healing even as we spoke in the late-afternoon light. Then as we were about to head back for dinner, a turtle's head emerged from the water right below our feet.

Now, I'm a Florida girl. I'm used to turtles. But this one was huge, the size of a sea turtle, its mammoth claws pawing the water to stick out the ugliest round head I'd ever seen.

We gasped at first. But our shock turned to delight as we watched it submerge, mesh with the moss at the bottom of the lake, and then swim back up again to the surface.

I took the turtle's visit as an affirmation. I was right where I needed to be.

My "advance" was working.

July 16, 2011

Camping with 9-year-old was magical trip

It's been over a month now since I took my 9-year-old daughter, Jenna, camping in North Carolina.

I can't think of those five days without my chest getting tight. Sometimes joy is so intense, it's slightly painful.

I was exactly 9 years old when I first went camping with my family. I felt as if I had entered a whole new world.

Growing up in a Chicago suburb, I rarely spent time in the woods, never saw a bubbling creek, seldom noticed the stars overhead.

So from that very first camping trip, I was hooked. My favorite childhood memories involved campfires, ice-cold swimming holes, mist rising from the Smoky Mountains, the smell of hamburgers on the grill.

But perhaps what I loved the most was hearing my parents laugh. They were more relaxed on those trips than they ever were at home.

For one reason or another — my health, my spouse's health, the bad economy — I've not taken Jenna camping much in the past. This year the stars seemed to align just right, and I decided to take her on a camping trip, just the two of us.

From the get-go, Jenna was the perfect companion. She was eager to do anything and loved my undivided attention.

She helped set up camp, was patient with my attempts to start a fire and even, with a little prodding, was willing to wash the dishes.

We were both challenged the day we trekked up to a fire tower near Standing Indian Campground. Dark clouds scudded overhead. Thunder rumbled. We barely made it back to the car before it started raining. Back at camp, we jumped into the tent.

Jenna was the first one to notice the leak. Just a few drips at first, then a steady stream. As lightning flashed and the tent shook from the wind, she shouted, "What are we going to do? What are we going to do?"

Forty-five minutes later, with the rain still coming down strong, I admitted defeat. We raced to the car, drove the 16 miles into town and got a hotel for the night. The next day we spent most of the day at the Laundromat drying our clothes.

But then we went back to the campsite. The sun came out. Our tent dried.

We continued with our adventure.

We took hikes, sloshed around waterfalls, jumped over creek rocks, cooked hotdogs over the fire. Every morning I'd make coffee and the two of us would walk around the campground.

One night she played with a group of seven boys who kept sneaking up to our campsite. She'd chase them away as they squealed with delight. Then they'd stealthily creep up to our site again.

At night, after she'd finally fall asleep in the tent, I would sit by the fire for a couple of hours and watch the flames. Slowly, the other campfires would die out, lanterns would turn off, campers would climb into their tent or trailer. The campground grew completely dark, except for one outdoor light by the bathroom; the only sounds were a few chirping crickets and the snap of a disintegrating fire log.

How much longer would Jenna want to be with me on a trip like this? Surely, by the time she was 12, her attitude would change. Mom wouldn't be so much fun anymore.

One day when we were hiking uphill, Jenna was ahead of me on the trail. Suddenly, she turned around, her face open with delight.

She must have noticed the bittersweet look on my face, because lickety-split, she raced down the trail, wrapped her arms around my waist and gave me a squeeze.

Then she was off again, scrambling up the hill, her bobbing head soon out of sight.

July 31, 2011

Pain, praise find expression in the psalms

The biblical psalms are cranky.

That's why I love them.

It's true that the better-known ones are full of praise for God. In fact, the word "hallelujah" is found almost exclusively in the Book of Psalms.

They also can be a tremendous source of comfort. Consider what is perhaps the most beloved psalm of all time, Psalm 23: *"The Lord is my shepherd, I shall not want. . . . Yea, though I walk through the valley of the shadow of death, I fear no evil, for thou art with me."*

But if you spend time with all 150 psalms, you'll find they're also steeped in the darker side of life — fear, anger, despair, abandonment. The psalmist sometimes feels numb to God's presence, at other times prods God to do the right thing.

"My God, by day I cry to you, but there is no answer." (Psalm 22:2)

"My wound oozes through the night and does not cease; my soul refuses comfort." (Psalm 77:3)

"Why, O Lord, do you stand aloof, heedless in times of trouble? . . . Rise, O Lord! Do not forget the lowly." (Psalm 10:1,12)

"I am bent and bowed; I walk about in gloom all day long. . . . I roar because of the turmoil in my mind." (Psalm 38:7-9)

"What can be gained from my death, from my descent into the Pit? Can dust praise You? Can it declare your faithfulness (Psalm 30:9)

"I am like a great owl in the wilderness, an owl among the ruins. . . . I am like a lone bird upon a roof." (Psalm 102:7-8)

Unlike Psalm 23, you won't find these psalm verses embroidered on wall hangings or shellacked on pieces of wood.

I was in my 20s when I fell in love with my first psalm verse. It was from Psalm 42: *"Like a doe who longs for running streams, so longs my soul for you, my God."*

That image depicted exactly how I felt at the time — young and wild, energy coursing through my veins, yearning for something to quench my spiritual thirst.

More than 20 years later, another psalm verse caused me to fall flat on my face. It was from Psalm 30: *"You lifted me from the pit; from the brink of the grave You brought me back to life."*

At the time, I was a three-year survivor of breast cancer. For the first year after diagnosis, I thought I was going to die. I'd look at my daughter, who was 3 at the time, and fear that I wouldn't be alive to celebrate her fifth birthday.

So when I read Psalm 30 during a Saturday morning service while on a retreat, it spoke directly to me.

For the time being, God was allowing me to live. I was so grateful, I went outside after the service, lay down on the grass and wept.

But it wasn't until this last year that I really dug into the psalms. Family health problems and economic concerns were absorbing most of my energy. I felt spiritually stagnant. The Jewish morning prayers that I had said for years suddenly weren't working for me.

So I turned to the psalms.

In the early-morning light, before the rest of my family was awake, I'd sit on the couch drinking green tea and read just one psalm a day. I'd reread it. Sometimes I'd read different translations of the same psalm.

After doing this for months, I came to appreciate the complexity and humanness of the psalms, to understand why they've been so important to people throughout the ages.

Unlike the rest of the Bible, where we might have to wrestle with whether it's literally true, or what it means, or how it applies to me, the psalms come straight from the heart.

At this time in my life, the crankiness of the psalms brings me a comfort. They allow me to express my despair, my confusion, my feelings of being overwhelmed. And I know I'm not alone.

We all feel like lone birds on a rooftop.

Reading the psalms helps me face that pain. Then afterward, bubbling up inside of me, comes a purer *hallelujah.*

Nov. 5, 2011

'So Whats' should review research about benefits of religion

On Jan. 8, the *Tallahassee Democrat* ran a story by *USA Today* reporter Cathy Lynn Grossman about the ongoing phenomenon of people dropping away from religion.

Only now, there's a new twist — a growing percentage of people don't even think about religion, much less talk about it. In one study, 44 percent spent no time seeking "eternal wisdom," and another 28 percent said, "It's not a priority in my life to find a deeper purpose."

This new subgroup of Americans are called the "So Whats."

Grossman quoted church historian Diana Butler saying: "We can't underestimate the power of the collapse of institutional religion in the first 10 years of this century. It's freed so many people to say they don't really care."

I've heard these kinds of statistics before, but they don't make sense.

That's because another arm of research has revealed the good news about religion — religious people are overwhelmingly healthier, happier, better connected to their communities, and more generous givers of both their time and money than their nonreligious counterparts. Just last month, I got another Pew Research Center report, "The

Civic and Community Engagement of Religiously Active Americans," basically saying the same thing.

So I'm confused. Religion — indeed the often derisively spoken of "organized religion — appears to be good for you. But more and more people want to have nothing to do with it?

Hmmmmmm.

Maybe it's like leading a healthy lifestyle. No other generation has been exposed to more information about the right things to eat, the benefits of exercise and the numerous ways to relieve stress.

But most of us say, in actions, if not in words, "Nah, not for me. It's not a priority in my life to be healthy."

You can lead a person to her broccoli, but you can't make her eat.

The sad part for the religious "So Whats" is that they don't even know what's available at the sumptuous table of faith.

Jan. 21, 2012

Are you picky or easily satisfied?

Are you a maximizer or a satisficer?

If you don't know what that means, once you do, you'll recognize yourself.

A maximizer is someone who always wants to get the best deal, who will spend countless hours comparing and thinking about any decisions.

Satisficers aren't so picky. They do a little comparing and then make a "good enough" decision.

Can you locate yourself? How about your spouse, parent or child?

I know I can. One of my favorite stories is about the time Terry and I were looking for tile when we were converting part of our carport into a bathroom. I volunteered to shop around.

I went to three or four stores, got the general price and style of the tiles in the market and brought home a sample of the one I liked the most — an inexpensive terra cotta 12x12-inch piece.

Terry wasn't crazy about it.

"Let me check out a few things," she said.

She spent two weeks visiting one store after another, bringing home tile after tile to compare them. I got so dizzy, I couldn't even remember which one cost what or where they were from.

Finally, one day she exclaimed "I found it!" and placed the tile proudly down on the table.

She picked the exact same one I had found in a day.

Now Joyce Ehrlinger, an assistant professor of psychology at FSU, and two others have delved into the maximizer/satisficer phenomenon more deeply and found that, once maximizers make a decision, they're not necessarily that invested in it.

"Because maximizers want to be certain they have made the right choice," the authors contend, "they are less likely to fully commit to a decision."

This goes against the normal grain. In most cases, once people own something, they like it more, Ehrlinger said. It reduces mental dissonance.

But maximizers aren't happy with their choices. In the study, the poster that maximizers got to pick out during the course of the research rarely found its way to a wall, unlike the satisficers, who hung it up.

"A week later, the maximizers were less likely to say they liked it," Ehrlinger said.

It's why maximizers don't like "All Sales Are Final" situations. They want to have the option of returning the purchased item.

Ehrlinger said she was interested in the research partly because of her own experience.

"I just bought a coffeemaker," she said. "I put time in not only deciding on the best coffeemaker, but on getting the best price. The hours I spent reading reviews and consumer reports was ridiculous."

The ongoing search can be depleting, she said, and have an impact when making major life choices, such as whom to marry and where to live.

It may be too simplistic to say that people are 100-percent maximizers or satisficers. But the phenomenon is real enough to provoke interesting discussion. At a recent holiday dinner with my extended family, I brought up

Ehrlinger's study, and everybody immediately knew which one he or she was.

Terry claims she's a maximizer during the deciding stage, but a satisficer once she makes a decision.

I can vouch for that.

She's always been happy with the terra cotta tile. And after almost three decades, she's still satisfied with me.

Jan. 29, 2012

Stopping rape starts with respecting women

The line in a recent *Tallahassee Democrat* made me want to scream: "It's kind of a football player thing."

The "thing" is leaving the bedroom door open — presumably so your roommates can watch you have sex.

That's what football player Chris Casher told investigators that he and Jameis Winston would do when they are with women.

Ugh.

Up until then, I had tried not to rush to judgment in the Winston case, although admittedly, I tend to believe women who say they've been raped. The real problem is women reporting rape, something like 60 percent.

But as a former journalist, I tried to keep an open mind, even as I winced when I read story after story in this newspaper about what a nice guy Winston is. As if nice guys don't sexually assault women.

A 2011 governmental survey reported that 1 in 5 American women have been sexually assaulted in their lifetimes.

In July, the World Health Organization, in a first-of-its-kind report, stated that 1 in 3 women around the world have experienced physical or sexual violence.

So if that many women are being assaulted, who is doing the assaulting? I'd like to know this statistic: One in how many men are perpetrators?

It's got to be a lot.

And I bet many of them are nice guys. Fathers, husbands, brothers, pastors, coaches.

People we know and love.

Which is why rape is my problem, it's your problem, it's all of our problem. The word is not getting through to our men that women deserve respect, sexual and otherwise. That should be a cultural norm, but it's not.

As I write this column, my 11-year-old daughter is listening to "Blurred Lines," by Robin Thicke. The beat is infectious, but the words stink.

I know you want it.

I know you want it.

I know you want it.

But you're a good girl.

Today I take the time to look up the lyrics, because I can't understand them all. And it gets worse, describing violent sex.

Not many women can refuse this pimpin', I'm a nice guy, but don't get it if you get with me.

There's that nice guy again, right there on my daughter's iPod.

How do we change this ugly part of our culture?

Ruth Krug, in a recent column, suggested that restorative justice, rather than just criminal proceedings, might be one way. Instead of going through the legal system, perhaps getting the accuser and accused in the same room and working through an incident might be better.

"The principles of restorative justice focus on honesty, respect, individual accountability and healing, rather than on incarceration and punishment," wrote Krug, herself a survivor of sexual violence. "The doors are opened for both sides involved in an incident to talk directly about the events and transgressions rather than leave it up to an adversarial and often impersonal legal system to resolve."

I'm not sure it would work, but it's an intriguing idea. It's got to be better than what's happened in the Winston case. When Winston didn't get charged, there seemed to be a collective, "Whew! That's over. Now we can get on with the Heisman Trophy and the national championship."

But we should insist that the social conversation continue. Rape doesn't start at the moment of physical contact. It starts in the mind of someone who sees the other person as less than human.

Listening to songs like "Blurred Lines" adds to this mind set. So does keeping bedroom doors open during sex.

The latter doesn't make Winston a rapist, but it makes him less than a gentleman.

It's hard to imagine a politician or celebrity making a racial slur and then being handed a national award. But disrespecting women doesn't seem to stand in the way.

The day it does, I'll know we're making real progress.

Dec. 21, 2013

We're so much better if we aren't alone

What do Americans need for the 21st century?

Last week, President Obama outlined his vision in his State of the Union speech, touching on everything from early childhood education to new IRAs. And, of course, he hit the steady drumbeat of jobs, jobs, jobs.

But one element was missing — one that supersedes money and paid work. It's people skills.

My biggest concern about my children's future doesn't involve the debt, climate change, Social Security or the job market — although these are all important. I worry that we don't know how to live together.

One-person households account for more than 1 in 4 homes in America. That's up from 1 in 6 in 1970 and 1 in 20 in 1900.

Eric Klinenberg, author of "Going Solo: The Extraordinary Rise and Surprising Appeal of Going Alone," warns us not to rush to judgment about this trend. Most of these folks, he says, choose to live alone and like it.

But I don't buy it. I suspect there will always be people who need to live alone — and who are their best selves when they do. But one-fourth of the population?

That's too many. I wonder if the numbers are high because we don't know how to negotiate 21st century relationships — particularly in close quarters.

I'm a part of that phenomenon as much as anyone. My kids have grown up hearing me complain, "I need some space!" I have a secret fantasy of living by myself, sitting in a room devoid of furniture or knickknacks, surrounded by a quiet, Zen-like atmosphere. Instead, I've settled for a room in my house that I've turned into my "girl cave." No one is allowed to come in without permission.

So I understand the modern need for control of space. The more we get, the more we want.

But the advantages of living with others are also compelling, whether you're living with family members or friends. It's cheaper and environmentally friendly (each of us doesn't have to have our own refrigerator, washing machine or air conditioner). It mitigates loneliness and the mercurial job market. It allows you to take care of someone and for someone to take care of you. It's an opportunity to share life's burdens, day to day.

I want this for my children.

So I wish Obama, or someone prominent, would raise this as a social concern. We should be talking about it on both a community and personal level. How can we bring people back together? What skills do we need to make living with others a success?

Looking to the past may not help us. Power structures within households a century ago are not the same as today. Women expect to be equal partners. Grown children aren't going to work the family farm or go into the family business. Young people are marrying later. Elders, who are living longer, have their own interests.

To work today, people sharing households will need excellent communication skills, a strict adherence to personal boundaries and a fairness ethic that extends to everyone.

Most of all, we need a place to practice these skills. If we live alone, that won't happen.

In the 14th century, a Sufi master wrote:

We should lean against each other more,
in such a strange world as this, that can make you scared.
We should support each other — give more warmth,
in such a demanding world as this.

In the 21st century, we still live in that strange, demanding world. We still need warmth and support and someone to lean into.

That happens best when we've living under the same roof.

Feb. 8, 2014

Think what churches could do

It's time to unleash the power of Tallahassee's interfaith community.

We've hosted plenty of joint services and panel discussions. We've worked together on projects such as Tallahassee Equality & Action Ministry (TEAM), now defunct, and the annual CROP Walk to feed the hungry.

But we have religious institutions on almost every corner here in town. If we pooled our resources, our impact would skyrocket.

We already have one great example — Manna on Meridian.

In 2009, two churches that are literally a stone's throw away from each other — St. Stephen Lutheran and Faith Presbyterian — decided to open a food pantry together. On one Saturday a month, they would give a bag of groceries to anyone who showed up, no questions asked.

Word got around fast, and soon they had long lines of people waiting for food. Within a year, two more churches on Meridian joined the effort. Today volunteers give out more than 230 bags of groceries in an hour.

The same thing can be done to help out struggling schools.

Some individual congregations have already adopted schools, providing everything from mentors to school supplies. That's what John Wesley United Methodist Church has done with Hartsfield Elementary, a school just down the street.

Judi McDowell, the volunteer coordinator for the school, is thrilled with the church's participation. But she admits the school could use more help. Hartsfield is a Title I school with a large number of students from low socioeconomic backgrounds.

If other nearby congregations joined with John Wesley, the impact could be tremendous. They could set a goal of making sure that every student who needed a mentor got one or that every student passed the FCAT.

But congregations don't have to be limited to schools or food pantries. They could focus on foster children, the elderly, animals, the environment. They could provide office space for nonprofits or other worthy groups.

Religious institutions already have the infrastructure — classrooms, gymnasiums, playgrounds, open land — which often doesn't get used during the week.

And they have the people power. Research shows that people in faith communities give more of their time and money to social causes than their secular counterparts.

Many seem to want to give more. As the faith editor of the *Tallahassee Democrat* for six years, I often heard the refrain, "We want to get out of the four walls of the sanctuary."

My impression was that these folks often didn't know what or how.

We could start by getting together with congregations in our area to discuss what we want to tackle. Perhaps it's a problem in a surrounding neighborhood or one that affects folks citywide. We could start a new program or add to an existing one.

In addition to providing a needed service, we would be building relationships with people of other faiths and denominations. Few things create intimacy faster than working together on a project. That's been true for Vicki

Weber, who coordinates more than 40 volunteers for Manna on Meridian. Getting to know people from other churches, she said, has been one of the best parts.

Sometimes when I drive around Tallahassee, I get goose bumps thinking about all the things the interfaith community could do together. We just need to get out of those four walls.

Feb. 21, 2014

Entertainment crosses the line to depravity

Characters' dark sides don't reflect reality

I stopped watching the TV series "Scandal" after a main character tied up a woman, forced her mouth open and pulled out her teeth.

In the second season of the "House of Cards," the main character abruptly shoved a journalist in front of an oncoming subway. Couldn't watch that one anymore, either.

Ditto for "Breaking Bad." After watching the third show, I just couldn't get past the idea that the schoolteacher main character was making methamphetamine.

Meth!

You know, that drug is so highly addictive, few people ever recover.

Some might say that these shows have dark, edgy, complicated characters. I say baloney.

These shows have no moral compass whatsoever.

The torturer in "Scandal" is totally accepted by the other characters. Even the beloved Olivia Pope, although she might get a slight frown of disapproval on her face, turns the other way.

Of course, Olivia has moral dilemmas of her own. She helps rig a presidential election. Then she has an affair with the married president. The viewers, I presume, are supposed to root for her, so that at least once a season, we get to watch these two have hot, steamy sex on the TV screen. Didn't we almost impeach a president for this kind of behavior?

In "House of Cards," I initially got reeled in. In fact, I watched all 13 episodes of Season One in about a week when they came out on Netflix last winter. I was intrigued by the politics in Washington (the same reason I started watching "Scandal"). Everyone knows all kinds of things go on behind the scenes, and this show was going to show me how a major political power broker worked his magic.

But by the end of the season, the power broker was a murderer, and almost every other character was pathetic or depraved. I wasn't going to watch it again, but when the second season came out recently, like a guilty addict, I turned it on.

My bad. After watching the young journalist get pushed to her death, I had a hard time falling asleep.

I know in "Breaking Bad" that it was just a literary device that got the schoolteacher to start making meth. He had inoperable lung cancer, so he wanted a quick way to make some cash to leave behind for his wife and child.

But I couldn't stop chastising him in my head. This is what you want your legacy to be? I've had cancer; so has my spouse. We now know hundreds of people who have had cancer. We all think about what we'll leave behind. Creating a drug that would ruin a person's life, especially a young person's, is not one of them.

So it doesn't matter to me if the acting is good, if the screenplay is original or if the humor is quirky. I can't watch it.

When I do, I feel as if I'm participating in a collective co-dependency. Co-dependents make excuses for the addicts in their lives. They downplay the damage addicts do. They become so accustomed to bad behavior, they don't even notice it anymore.

What bothers me the most in these shows is that so many of the characters are twisted. I don't believe that reflects reality. Yes, we all have our dark sides. And, yes, we sometimes compromise our values.

But most of us struggle to do the right thing.

I, for one, look to film to help me figure that out. When the main characters are making meth, torturing people and having illicit affairs — and as a viewer I'm almost cheering them on or am expected to overlook that behavior — it doesn't help. I don't feel informed, challenged or even entertained. I get either agitated or filled with despair.

So I'm not going to tune into these shows, no matter how tempting it is to see what Olivia is going to do next or whether that Washington power broker ever gets caught.

I still have the power to just say no.

March 10, 2014

A few people help make a city great

Cascades Park might inspire you to pitch in

I've been to Cascades Park three times in the past week or so. I can't seem to stay away.

I love the winding sidewalks, the rolling landscapes, the gushing waterfall, the Canada geese that are already claiming the stream that runs through it. When, on the first full day it was open, I watched children giggle and prance around the jets of water springing up from the pavement, my heart filled with gratitude — gratitude for all the hearts and hands and planning that went into making this park happen.

Because, frankly, I had nothing to do with it.

I'm not alone, according to Peter Kageyama, author of "For the Love of Cities," who came to Tallahassee last year. He says that, in most cities, only 1 percent of the population is responsible for making things that the rest of us enjoy. Most of us, he says, are just consumers.

We take from its resources: parks, security, airports, roads and bike paths. Most of us consume the city without giving back, other than by being good citizens who obey laws, pay their taxes and, as a byproduct of consumption, spend money back into the community.

This certainly is true of me when it comes to city parks and greenways. For decades, for example, I've gone to Lake Ella, watching each of my three children scramble up the famous "climbing tree." I watched as new trees were planted, the gazebo was built, the stands for doggy "poop" bags were put in place. Other people made those things happen. I just enjoyed them.

Around New Year's, I walked six miles in the Miccosukee Greenway. The paths were beautifully laid out, benches were placed in strategic scenic areas, bird houses were attached to poles, the large expanses of grass were mowed. I've never helped. But it was available when I got ready to take my hike.

Even Koucky Park, the sweet out-of-the-way green space across the street from my house, I've had little to do with. Somebody, at some time, made sure this little neighborhood jewel was made available to the public. Over the years, a series of other people have mowed the grass, fixed the fence near the road and repaired the bridge over the creek. I just visit.

So, OK, the building of Cascades Park seemed to go on forever. And, yes, we have ongoing issues involving noise levels and keeping kids off the Korean War Memorial. But this park is going to be enjoyed by so many people over so many years that the good it will do the community is incalculable.

The largeness of it, the physicality of it, inspires me to become part of that 1 percent, to help create things in this town that benefit people outside my small circle of family and friends. Kageyama says that even increasing those numbers by a small amount will have tremendous impact on the community.

To do this, he says, we need to move from just being attached to our hometown to falling in love with it.

Cascades Park has helped me fall a little deeper in love with Tallahassee. So to begin with, whenever I go there, I'm going to follow the spiritual practice some people do before eating food. They pause and think about all the people who helped bring that meal to the table: the farmer who planted the seeds or raised the chicken, the people who harvested or butchered the food, the truck drivers who brought it to the grocery store, the cooks who turned it into a meal. It took many, many hands to bring that food to their plate.

So it is with Cascades Park. Many people, most of whom I don't know, made this place possible for me.

I will make sure I pause long enough to say "Thanks."

March 31, 2014

Sometimes there's virtue in just listening

Most of us live in political silos, talking and socializing only with people who agree with us.

Even when information from the "other side" does manage to penetrate our world, research says we rarely change our minds.

So why pretend that going to a panel discussion of people on both sides of the political divide will make any difference?

Because while more information might not affect us, building a relationship with someone on the other side might.

That's what the folks at The Village Square have been banking on for the past eight years. The organization was born out of the polarization that occurred over the proposed coal plant in 2005.

The founders — one liberal, the other a conservative, who were on opposite sides of the coal plant— deplored how contentious the social conversation had gotten around the issue. They started The Village Square, hoping that bringing people with diverse viewpoints together for civil discussion would improve our democracy.

They struck a nerve. The packed crowds that show up to most Village Square events demonstrate that people are hungry for this kind of discourse.

I know I am.

That's why I've attended many of the events, including the most recent Dinner at the Square titled "7 Deadly Sins: The decline of moral community and the rise of public corruption." The idea was that conservatives care about the moral behaviors of individuals and communities, while liberals focus on morals in the political sphere.

The speakers were Bill Shiell, pastor of the 165-year-old First Baptist Church downtown, and Lucy Morgan, a Pulitzer Prize-winning journalist who covered state politics for decades for the *Tampa Bay Times* (formerly the *St. Petersburg Times*).

Being a liberal, I agreed with everything Morgan had to say. I cheered when she talked about nailing corrupt law-enforcement officials and politicians. I nodded in approval when she said the recent court rulings allowing people to contribute whatever they wanted to political committees corrupted the election process. I bemoaned with her the decline in newspapers and the Florida counties that no longer had a watchdog newspaper covering local government decisions.

But, surprisingly, I found myself agreeing with a lot of what Shiell said, too. Yes, my teeth were set on edge when he talked about how Christians needed to separate people from their actions — in other words, love the sinner but hate the sin.

Lesbians and gays have heard that one before. It's just insulting.

But many of his other views were similar to mine. He questioned the idea of private morality — that how you acted in your private life wasn't anybody's business. He claimed that whether we want it to or not, everything we do affects other people.

This was a loaded statement, and we could argue for hours about who, then, gets control of what — but he hit on a spiritual truth. We're all connected, and you can't separate yourself from the consequences of your behavior, even if the law allows you to.

Shiell didn't excuse or minimize church scandals, either, saying they negatively impact congregations and the public at large. But he also spoke eloquently about what the faith community can offer the larger society — perhaps the strongest one being a place where different generations meet together at least once a week. In our often age-segregated society, this is a rare opportunity.

Religious congregations are also a breeding ground for service, he said, both for young people and for adults. The first responders after a disaster, for example, often come from the faith community.

When asked how we can heal the deep political divides in our country, he suggested we start by focusing on our children. People of all political persuasions want the best for their children, he said. Perhaps if we started there, we'd have a better chance of solving the problems we all face.

I suspect at election time, Shiell and I will vote very differently. Nothing he said changed any particular view I had on an issue. But listening to him speak did allow me to connect with him personally. He seemed level-headed, concerned, approachable.

For two hours, I managed to get out of my silo. The view wasn't so bad.

April 16, 2014

Human element outlasts memory

It happens every time.

Someone may be laughing or singing or even flirting, and the boundaries between volunteer and client melt away. We're just humans together, connecting.

I wasn't expecting that when I started volunteering three years ago at the Good Friends Social Club, a joint program of the Alzheimer's Project and Temple Israel. Once a week, the daylong respite program gives caregivers a break while volunteers provide activities for their loved ones.

The biggest connection often comes when we sing. The clients all love the old songs and show tunes — "Let Me Call You Sweetheart," "Hello, Dolly," "Hey, Good-Lookin'" and "On Top of Old Smokey." Most people belt out the songs with gusto. While many can't remember what they had for breakfast, they can often sing all the verses of "Amazing Grace."

I remember one man who can't even talk anymore. He has a hard time doing the art projects, playing bingo or stretching during yoga. But when the song leader starts singing an old jazz tune, his face suddenly brightens, and he drums his fingers on the table and mouths a few words. Then he looks across the table at me and smiles.

A few minutes later he sinks back into silence, his memory of that moment already gone. But his smile continues to glow in me.

The clients also love to be around children. In the morning, a group of kids from Temple Israel preschool called the Forget-Me-Nots come to sing for them. Again, the somber-faced woman who is slowly drinking her coffee suddenly starts grinning. The clients look at each other and laugh. One day, after the singing is over, a man turns to me with a twinkle in his eye and says, "Our future is secure."

Another day, everyone sits in a circle, and the coordinator throws a huge, blowup beach ball into the middle. It's like the electricity is suddenly turned on. People are kicking and throwing the ball at one another, the laughter nonstop. People who can't coordinate their hands and legs to do chair yoga can at least kick the ball. No one zones out during this activity.

I'm also surprised at the flirting. One woman lights up when a man walks into the room. Invariably, she finds a way to sit down next to him.

Others carry on a repartee across the table, oblivious to others around them. Some walk, arms linked, across the room.

Perhaps most touching is how they help one another. A woman who can walk helps another woman who is having a hard time move from the table to the yoga chair. They help each other find the numbers on the bingo card. One woman makes sure the woman next to her has enough to eat.

So even as our memory fades, our hands and limbs lose function, our speech disappears, we hold on for as long as we can to our human connections. We respond to music, to children, to a little romance in the air.

Even if it lasts for only a moment.

May 2, 2014

Me and my little Aliner

For years I've insisted that camping is superior to going to motels.

My wife says otherwise. As you might have guessed, we've done very little camping in the past 30 years.

But that's about to change. For my midlife crisis, I bought a hard-sided, A-frame pop-up called an Aliner. I'm absolutely in love. It sets up in about 60 seconds, keeps me off the ground at night and dry in the rain.

Goodbye, sterile-smelling hotel rooms and who-knows-what's-been-on-this motel bedspread. This little pop-up was going to allow me to be adventurous. A regular wild woman!

I soon made plans for a solo three-day trip to St. Andrews State Park on Panama City Beach. But I had one little problem. I didn't know how to backup the Aliner.

No problem, I tried to reassure myself. Tons of other people have done it.

So a few days before I set off for the beach, I went to an empty parking lot off Old St. Augustine Road to practice. I turned the wheel one way. Nope, too far. Then the other way. That didn't work either. Back and forth, back and forth. I'd stop, pull forward, try again. After an hour, drenched in sweat, I called it a day.

It wasn't until I got out of the car that I noticed a foot-long dented gash in my left rear fender. Took the wind right out of my wild woman sails. But I figured, if I took my time once I got to the campground, I'd have learned enough to back it up into the campsite.

Wishful thinking.

When I got there, I found my campsite and drove a little past it to position myself to back up. A blond-haired boy in sunglasses, about 8 years old, got off his bicycle to watch me.

I started to back up. No, not that way. I pulled forward, backed up again.

The boy stood there, head cocked to one side, hand on his hip. I tried to ignore him.

After several more backing-up attempts, a woman came over to see if I needed help.

"Let me get my daddy," she said. "He's a truck driver and can back anything up."

And, of course, he did. In less than three minutes, he maneuvered the Aliner deftly into place.

OK, I thought. I unhitched the Aliner from the car, popped up the camper in seconds, plugged in the electricity. My plan was to put on the air conditioner, sit in the camper and gather my wits.

But the air conditioner pumped out nothing but hot air. I pressed this button, that button, every which way, until I had to admit it just wasn't working. By now it was 90 degrees in there.

Grrr. For months I had been telling people that I was getting the air conditioner for Terry. She wouldn't come camping with me without it, I'd say, implying that I was much tougher. I didn't need such luxuries. Now here I was, almost undone because it wouldn't work.

I snapped open my folding chair in disgust and sat down under a tree. Maybe I could make it through the night if I at least had a fan. I drove off for the nearest Wal-Mart.

That night, with the fan blowing directly on me, I cooled down and fell into a deep sleep. The next day it was like a curtain had lifted. My troubles were behind me.

I walked down to the boardwalk in the morning light, watching boats. The breeze from the bay kept me cool. I saw two dolphin fins arch out of the water not more than 20 feet away. I watched the pair dive and resurface several times, listening as their air holes released soft spurts of breath.

I spent hours sitting at my campsite, with the fan — attached to a long extension cord I also managed to buy at Wal-Mart — right by my side. I read my book, day-dreamed, looked up at the cloudless sky. Birds flew among the trees, coming and going for hours.

I didn't go to the beach until almost 5 p.m. Only a few of us were left on the sand, and a couple of surfers were in the water. The sun slanted sideways, casting shadows on the waves. I stood knee-deep in the surf as wave after wave came in.

It was almost dark when I came back to my site. When I looked up, I saw three does in the bushes, searching for food. One lifted her head, looked at me and gave a short wiggle with her tail. They were quiet and unafraid, moving stealthily from bush to bush. I had time to take in their long, narrow noses, their spindly legs, the patch of white underneath their tails.

Then suddenly, they were gone, disappearing into the underbrush. I sat in my chair until it was completely dark.

In the morning, I went outside to heat water for coffee. As I unlatched the top of my Coleman stove, a green frog jumped out, startling me. Looking down, I noticed a dozen more all over the bottom of the stove.

That's when I decided it was definitely worth the trip. Dolphin breath, swirling birds, deer at dusk, frogs in the morning. You're never going to experience that in a hotel room.

July 20, 2014

There's a special magic in breaking bread together

July 24 was a banner human rights day for me.

In the morning, I was at the Capitol delivering marriage equality petitions to Florida State Attorney General Pam Bondi. At nightfall, I broke a Ramadan fast at Temple Israel with a group of Muslims, Christians and Jews.

These actions represent two potent models of creating change: political confrontation and breaking bread together.

The older I get, the more I prefer the latter.

Still, I agreed to go with several other couples to Bondi's office to urge her to withdraw her appeal of a recent ruling by a Monroe County judge allowing gays to marry in Key West.

My enthusiasm was moderate at best. Not because I was discouraged — I'm confident that marriage equality is coming. Bondi is one of the last holdouts in this tidal wave of change.

I'm just tired of knocking on this door.

Terry and I had a commitment ceremony in 1986, were legally married in Toronto in 2004 and last year signed up for the Leon County Domestic Partner Registry. It's time to just be really, truly, legally married, instead of being in this piecemeal, sort-of limbo.

But my mood suddenly brightened right near the end when two young men were interviewed by reporters.

Unlike the other gay couples — older lesbians who had been together for decades — these men had been partners for five years and wanted to start a family. But, they said, they wanted to do it in the right order — get married first, then have kids.

I had to smile. They were using conservative language to humanize their own situation.

I told them that when they finally do get married in Florida, I hope I'm invited to the wedding.

Later that day, I sat at a table equally divided among Muslims, Christians and Jews. We were there to break the fast during one of the remaining nights of Ramadan, a month when Muslims fast from sunup to sundown. The dinner was sponsored by the Atlantic Institute, an organization dedicated to facilitating dialogue and bridging cultures from both sides of the Atlantic.

We listened to leaders of all three faiths talk about how their religions dealt with thanksgiving. We listened to a taped portion of the Quran, and then to an Islamic prayer.

Finally, when nightfall was officially declared, we feasted on what had to be the best dinner served that night in Tallahassee — chicken, salmon, rice, salad, dates, grape leaves, mashed potatoes and mounds of baklava.

So many people were talking to others at their tables, it was hard to hear. It was an unabashed success.

The only thing that would have made it truly amazing is if Palestinian Muslims had been there. But the recent conflict in Gaza made that unlikely.

The latest round of fighting happened shortly after the kidnapping and slaying of three Israeli teenagers in June. I try not to imagine the last hours or minutes of those boys' lives. My oldest son spent four months in Israel when he was 16 — the age of two of the victims. If this happened to him . . . my mind can't even go there.

Sometime before the Ramadan dinner, I read that about 500 Palestinians and 30 Israelis had already died in the conflict. These figures were horrifying enough, but it was when I read the next statistic that my mind again stopped cold — of those 500 Palestinians, 70 were children.

Seventy. The size of my daughter's entire middle-school class.

The reasons for the conflict — on either side — suddenly didn't matter. All I could feel, for one horrible, heart-wrenching moment, was the grief of the parents.

So, no, I don't think Jews and Palestinians sitting down for a dinner would work right now. The tension would be too great, the grief too thick.

But that doesn't mean, like Martin Luther King Jr., that I can't have a dream, a dream that someday, in my lifetime, Jew and Palestinian, Pam Bondi and those two young men, I and a host of people I now fear, will sit down at the same table. We will laugh, talk, eat scrumptious food.

And our children will hold hands.

Aug. 3, 2014

Start now to stop campus assaults

Fall semester starts this week. But so does something more sinister: the Red Zone.

That's the time between now and the Thanksgiving holiday when there's typically a spike in sexual assaults, especially among freshman women.

According to the Centers for Disease Control, 19 percent of female undergraduates are assaulted during their college years. Many of the assaults happen in the fall.

Is this true at FSU? FAMU? TCC?

We don't know for sure. But legislation introduced in the U.S. Senate this summer would require colleges to conduct an annual anonymous survey to find out — and then publish the results online.

I'd love to see that.

Just as we annually track statistics on infant mortality in our county, we could track the number of sexual assaults of college students. Knowing the statistics may not change anything in and of itself, but it would keep the issue before us instead of waiting for some high-profile case to get everyone's attention.

But let's just say the 19 percent holds true for our town. With roughly 70,000 college students in Tallahassee every year — and about half of them being female — that means more than 6,000 college women have been or will be sexually assaulted. All but a few go unreported.

In the next few weeks, FSU is expected to announce what the university will be doing to beef up its focus on sexual assault. Interim President Garnett Stokes already has agreed to hire two sexual violence prevention coordinators this year.

Two men's groups — Men Advocating Responsible Conduct (MARC) at FSU and Men of Strength (MOST) at FAMU — have already popped up in recent years to address sexual violence.

But I have to say, as the mother of two young men, my first thought when I hear these high numbers is that there's been a parenting failure. While our daughters are the victims, our sons are the perpetrators.

Granted, the percentage is probably small. Some research suggests that 3 percent of college men are responsible for 90 percent of the rapes. But even if that's true, that means that, at any given time, more than 1,000 of them are roaming around on Tallahassee campuses.

When my oldest son went off to college seven years ago, I wish I had talked with him more about sexual violence. I remember having the "No means No" conversation, but that was about all. When I asked him recently about what he thought of that conversation, he said he didn't even remember it! He was also surprised that I thought we should have had more direct talks about sexual violence. He didn't need to be told, he said, how to be a decent human being.

That may be true. But there's more to preventing rape than just not being a rapist yourself.

There is now a strategy called bystander intervention — what you can do when you see a bad situation about to happen, perhaps at a party or a bar. Maybe you see someone who is very intoxicated being led into a bedroom, or you notice a guy cornering a woman in a hallway. You might talk with the woman, offering to bring her home, or tell the guy to back off. These kinds of interventions may be more effective than anything parents or college officials can do.

My son said that, now that he's 25 years old, he could see himself using these strategies — and, in fact, has removed a friend from a dangerous situation more than once. But he questions whether he could have done that at 18 or 19.

Maybe not. But if he had been educated about how to anticipate these situations, it might have given him more confidence.

No one knows yet whether bystander intervention actually prevents assaults, according to a recent White House Task Force. But what have been effective are two programs geared toward middle- and high-school students: "Safe Dates" and "Shifting Boundaries." Students in both programs meet during 10 sessions to cover everything from social attitudes and norms to the creation of plays and poster campaigns.

To me, this implies that, as parents, we should be having these conversations with our children way before they set off for college.

I also hope Tallahassee universities take note: Programs need to be in-depth and happen over the course of several months. What the Task Force said doesn't work is "brief, one-session educational programs conducted with college students."

The community at-large can also do more. We could paint the town red for sexual violence awareness the way we paint it pink for breast cancer. It would be so refreshing if men took the lead on this.

Starting in mid-August, we could have billboards all over town that read "No means No." Bars and restaurants could provide sexual violence literature — not just in women's bathrooms, but in men's. Coaches could talk to their athletes; fraternity brothers to one another. Clergy could give sermons on it. People all over town could wear red ribbons.

We don't have to wait for university officials or legislators to do something. We can start, right now, on making our town an assault-free zone.

Aug. 27, 2014

First camping trip brings laughter

We were only a few miles off Interstate 81 in southwest Virginia when Terry's Internet service went dead.

This wasn't a good sign. We had another 30 miles to go before we got to Grayson Highlands State Park, a remote campground in rural Virginia. We had reservations for a week.

A look of horror swept across Terry's face as the full impact hit her. "I can't be this far from civilization!" she cried, glancing helplessly at her iPhone.

I stayed quiet. It had never occurred to me to worry about cellphone connection. The last time I had done much camping, iPhones hadn't even been invented.

As we drove the winding roads, our A-frame popup camper towed behind us, Terry found the landscape outside our car windows turning sinister. The streets were wet, and gray clouds hunkered like angry monster shadows overhead. There wasn't another car in sight.

When she spotted a dead deer on the side of the road, she was into full Internet withdrawal.

"It's a bad omen!" she gasped. "All the other deer we've seen so far have been alive!"

By the time we got to the campground, it was almost dark. No one was at the office, but our reservation papers were clipped to the outside window. We slowly circled the almost deserted campground searching for a site.

When Terry finally decided on one, I opened the popup, already thinking about that glass of red wine I was going to have. But instead, a foul smell hit both of us so hard, we almost gagged. Something was rotting inside the camper.

"Here, smell over here!" Terry said, pointing to the top of the air conditioner vent. I sniffed. Sure enough, the smell was coming from that area. My heart sank. Was it a dead rat that had somehow gotten caught in there? How were we going to get it out? We couldn't sleep inside the camper with that smell.

I walked over to the picnic table to gather my wits. A minute later, Terry emerged from the camper clutching a dripping plastic bag of potatoes.

"I found what it was," she said, her nose crinkling.

Rule No 1: Never take potatoes on a camping trip and leave them in a closed-up camper all day.

We went into high gear, whipping out all the contents of the cabinet, dunking cans of food into a bin of sudsy water, scrubbing and scrubbing and scrubbing the bottom of the cabinet with Clorox wipes.

It was completely dark when we were finished. Rain pattered on the top of the camper. We looked at each other in relief.

Then I remembered: We still needed to get rid of the rotten bag of potatoes. We couldn't just leave it outside for the bears.

Of course, we didn't know where the garbage bin was. But we put on our raincoats, stuck the stinking mess into another plastic bag and jumped in the car. We circled the pitch-black campground, craning our necks, looking for the damn garbage bin.

I felt like I was a murderer in one of my favorite mystery novels, a bag of body parts bumping against my feet. How could I get rid of them?

Finally, we spotted the garbage bin and I hopped out, holding the reeking potatoes in front of me. Terry shined a flashlight on me so I could see. I tried to open the top of the bin, but there was an extra bar there to keep the bears out. It only opened a few inches.

As the rain poured down, I stuffed the potatoes through the 3-inch crack, pushing and shoving until I heard them clunk down inside.

Free at last! Time to get out of here!

Back at the camper we laughed so hard we could hardly breathe. The creepy, winding roads. The dead deer. The rotten potatoes. Our giggles would subside, only to erupt again, breaking loose like busted balloons.

"Sh-hh-hhh!" I admonished Terry. Noises in campgrounds travel far.

But it took us another 15 minutes before we could stop.

The next morning, when I went outside to heat water for coffee, I noticed a dark blob in one of the bins we used for washing dishes. Usually we empty them before we go to bed, but the night before had been so hectic, we forgot.

The blob turned out to be a drowned mouse, lying on its side. I reared back, but then came closer for a better look, taking in its delicate ears, its tiny claws.

When I showed it later to Terry, she looked at me in disgust. Another bad omen?

But it wasn't.

We had many stellar moments on our trip. One was two days after the potato fiasco when we were riding bikes on the Virginia Creeper Trail, cycling through countryside, over burbling creeks, the temperature a cool 76 degrees. We tubed down the Chattahoochee River in Helen, Georgia, ate fabulous food on a walking tour in Roanoke, Virginia, met a wonderful 12-year-old boy in Fairy Stone State Park who chatted with us as we sat by the fire. We saw tons of deer, spectacular mountain views and the wonderful faces of the friends and family members we visited.

But nothing will remain as vivid to us as our first time at Grayson. For years to come, we will be reliving that experience — the night that laughter washed away our fears.

Aug. 31, 2014

Use High Holy Days to consider the Holy Land

Today, on Rosh Hashana, the Jewish New Year, and 10 days from now on Yom Kippur, the Day of Atonement, Jews will recite a dramatic, heart-wrenching prayer called the "Unetaneh Tokef."

Who shall live and who shall die . . .
Who shall perish by fire and who by water
Who by sword and who by beast . . .
Who by strangling and who by stoning . . .

This year, these words can't help but evoke images of the recent war in Israel and Gaza. By this time next year, how many more people will die by rocket or by airstrike, by kidnapping or by falling rubble?

A common reaction to this conflict is to want to blame one side or the other. People have spent decades going back and forth about this, to the point where some won't talk about it anymore because they're left feeling one of two ways: angry or hopeless.

So this High Holy Day season, I'm not going to ask the question: Who is responsible? Instead, my faith, and the many prayers recited during the season, call me to ask, "How do I respond to this tragedy as an individual?"

Here are my commitments for the coming year. The first is to become more educated. I've already read a lot about the history of the Israeli–Palestinian conflict and keep up with the news, but I've learned that you never can know enough. This conflict has so many levels and nuances that, anytime I think I have a good grasp of the issues, I learn something else that sheds more light.

The second commitment is to increase my involvement with Palestinians and people in the Muslim community. I was recently inspired to do this by an article in *The New York Times* about a program in Maine called Seeds for Peace. For the past 22 years, this organization has brought together hundreds of teenagers from conflict regions in the world — particularly Israel and the Palestinian territories — for three weeks during the summer. In addition to eating, sleeping and playing games together, they have daily discussions about the conflicts in their home countries.

According to the two researchers who wrote the article, participants in the program showed an increase of positive feelings for the other group and a greater willingness to work for peace after attending the camp. A year later, they continued to report similar attitudes.

The researchers also found that "the campers who were able to form just one close relationship with someone from the other group were the ones who developed the most positive attitudes toward the other group. Indeed, forming one friendship was as good or better a predictor of future attitudes toward the other group than the total number of friendships that a person formed."

Building a friendship with one person — that's something I can do.

My final commitment is to support those people and organizations that are willing to grapple with the complexity of this problem and not just make it into an either/or situation. Some people have strong opinions on this issue, and the media highlight that so much, it's difficult to even broach the subject. (Check out the Jon Stewart video clip "We need to talk about Israel." Stewart barely utters the word "Israel" when he's attacked from all sides, with the last person shouting, "Self-hating Jew!")

One step I've already taken is watching the documentary "The Gatekeepers." It's about the Israeli internal security service, the Shin Bet, through the eyes of six of its past leaders. These are the guys responsible for tracking down terrorists.

I was particularly moved by what Yuval Diskin, who was a head of the Shin Bet from 2005 to 2011, said at the very beginning of the film. I'm going to quote him extensively to show how he wrestles with this difficult situation:

"As head of the Shin Bet, you learn that politicians prefer binary options. . . . They want you to tell them, 'Zero or one. Do it. Don't do it.'

"As a commander, I find myself in situations that are different shades of gray. Let's say you are hunting a terrorist. You can get him but there are one or two other people in the car. You're not sure if they're part of his gang or not.

"What do you do? Do you fire or not? There is no time. These situations last seconds, minutes at most. People expect a decision, and by decision they usually mean 'to act.' That's a decision. 'Don't do it' seems easier, but it's often harder.

"Sometimes it's a super-clear operation. No one hurt except the terrorists. Even then, later, life stops, at night, in the day, when you're shaving. We all have our moments. . . . You say, 'OK, I made a decision and X number of people were killed. They were definitely about to launch a big attack. No one was near them. It was as sterile as possible.'

"Yet you still say, 'There's something unnatural about it.' What's unnatural is the power you have to take three people, terrorists, and take their lives in an instant."

Who shall live and who shall die.
Who decides?
Sometimes it's in God's hands. Sometimes it's in ours.

Sept. 25, 2014

Women must get past being objects

For the most part, I ignore pop culture.

Ever since I became a feminist in my early 20s, I haven't liked the way it portrays women, so I've minimized my contact with TV, women's magazines, shopping malls and music videos.

But I now have a 12-year-old daughter — and I've been forced to take a closer look. What I've found is uglier than I would have imagined.

It started with listening to the radio, which my daughter flips on every time we get in the car. I've been astonished by the lyrics — ones I had assumed were not played on FM radio.

Last December I wrote about the sexually violent lyrics of "Blurred Lines" by Robin Thicke. What I didn't do was watch the video. Until recently. I about fell out of my chair. Naked women literally prance around a fully clothed Thicke like, well, there's no better way to say it, like slut puppies.

Then I watched "Wrecking Ball" by Miley Cyrus. Watching her swing naked on a ball and salaciously lick a sledge hammer made me cringe.

But it's when I watched Nicki Minaj's "Anaconda" that I wanted to cry.

This is where the women's movement has gotten us?

One of the rallying cries of the movement in the 1960s and '70s was that we didn't want to be portrayed as sexual objects. I assumed high heels, the emphasis on makeup and being scantily clad would become a thing of the past.

How wrong I was.

It seems the more women achieve, the more stringent the standards of beauty become — one must be skinnier, sexier, smoother, younger than ever before.

But the above-mentioned videos — and J Lo's new "Booty" video that I just watched — take this to an absurd extreme. They're all about women looking "sexually ready" for the viewer.

This is not robust female sexuality. This is playing to the camera. This is caricature. This is pornography, pure and simple.

We're so used to it, we don't even notice.

I caught a women's talk show that discussed the new J Lo video, and what did they focus on? How the video showed that "sexy" doesn't have an age cutoff.

Nothing about the appropriateness of it. Nothing about how these images affect our daughters.

Somehow we get that Jameis Winston standing on a table in the FSU union and yelling something nasty about women is offensive, but we don't call it vulgar when a woman flashes her butt to the camera over and over, encouraging the viewer to do just what Winston described. Why aren't we enraged about that?

Instead, women absorb these bizarre sexualized standards, consciously or unconsciously.

It's the reason most of us don't like our bodies — about 90 percent of us, according to some studies. And the more we consume pop culture in the form of TV, advertisements, women's magazines and music videos, the more self-critical we are, according to the "Report of the APA Task Force on the Sexualization of Girls," a must-read for all parents.

And it's getting worse.

Advertising with females as "decorative objects," such as a woman standing in front of a car, has increased since the women's movement. Images of women naked or in semi-undress have skyrocketed. Sexual harassment in TV shows — up. Sexual content in music videos — up.

One telling example is the study that examined the diaries of adolescent girls over 100 years. In the early years, girls focused on improving their studies and becoming more well-mannered, whereas in the last 20 years, girls focused almost exclusively on their physical appearance.

The APA report calls this self-objectification, a process in which girls, picking up on the social advantages of being sexy, such as popularity, internalize the standards and begin policing their own — and other women's — bodies. They constantly see themselves through other people's eyes, evaluating their physical desirability.

No one needs to force us to be sexual objects. We do it to ourselves.

Which is both the bad news and the good news. Bad because these standards are so embedded in our psyche that many of us insist that we want to do all these things. Good because, if we want, we can make it stop.

So I'm not going to ban all offensive-sounding songs from my car radio (although there are ones I just refuse to listen to). My thumbs can't stop up this dam. When I asked my daughter, for instance, if she'd seen the Miley Cyrus video, she said that someone at school had shown it to her.

So while I can't stop the flood of images or lyrics, I will, over and over again, help her understand that sexual objectification is something she can support or not support — at least in her own consumer consumption. I will not make comments about my own or another woman's body. I will support her athletic abilities, her need for adventure, her growing competence in a zillion areas of her life.

The APA report suggested other ways to counteract sexualization — including media literacy training, comprehensive sex education, participation in sports and extracurricular activities, religious and spiritual instruction, the creation of alternative media and social activism.

Women will be truly free only when we can say, without hesitation, that we love our bodies. That's the freedom I want for my daughter.

Oct. 10, 2014

Mind your own busyness

Have you ever been guilty of being "busier than thou"?

I know I have.

That's because busyness has become the new status symbol by which we evaluate ourselves and others.

In her new book, "Overwhelmed: Work, Love, and Play When No One Has the Time," Brigid Schulte writes that, by the end of the 20th century, researchers found that busyness was "not just a way of life, but glamorous. . . . It's a sign of high social status."

It's gotten to the point where many of us even brag about busyness. You can hear the one-upmanship anytime parents get together. We list all the activities our kids are involved in, how jammed our weekends are, how there's no time for ourselves. We sigh, moan a little, shake our heads.

But nobody talks about how to cut down.

"As a culture, we have translated speed into a virtue," said Edson Rodriguez, a sociologist who studies frenetic families. "If you are busy, if you get things done quickly, if you move quickly throughout the day, it expresses success. . . . The feeling is, if I'm not busy, something's wrong."

A woman at my synagogue once asked me how I was doing, and I launched into how tired I was, rattling on about everything I was doing.

She looked at me and frowned. "You always tell me that you're tired."

That stopped me cold. I hadn't realized that I had been repetitive. I also thought, "If that's true, why aren't I doing something about it?"

As I looked deeper, I realized I was secretly proud of my busyness.

But I was also aware that busyness didn't necessarily equate with productivity, and it surely didn't increase my quality of life. Much of what I was doing was pure "busy work."

Today two things help me "get off the grid" of over-scheduling. The first is the experience I've gained from raising children far apart in age. The second is observing the Sabbath.

When I had my first child 25 years ago, I couldn't distinguish between what was important to do and what wasn't. Deciding how long to breast-feed, when he should start day care, what activities he should sign up for, what cultural events he should attend, occupied a lot of my time. I talked with other mothers about this constantly. We didn't want to make a mistake.

But because my two other children were born six and 13 years after my first one, I got a chance to see what effect those oh-so-important decisions had before making them a second and third time. What I discovered was — not much.

In general, you need to support your children's interests. In general, they need a good family life. Those things do make an impact.

But all those soccer games, violin lessons and summer camps weren't all necessary. My oldest son would have still grown up to be the wonderful man he is if he had only done about a third of them. Ditto for my second child.

So now with my daughter, the only child still at home, I don't feel angst about these issues anymore. She's on a soccer team and goes to religious school outside of her regular school hours. That's about it.

This fall, we decided not to sign her up for the cross country team — even though she's a great runner. We tried it last year, and it exhausted everybody. I dreaded Tuesdays, when I had to pick her up from track practice, zip her to a fast-food restaurant for dinner and then scurry over to the soccer field. Wednesdays were the same, only we ended up at Hebrew school instead of the soccer field.

So now, instead of driving around town, my daughter has more time to take the dogs down to the park, we eat together more at home, we're not as tired at the end of the week.

On Shabbat (the Jewish Sabbath) I also don't work, go shopping or do housework. I'm not 100-percent faithful on this, but it's true more times than not.

I spend the day with family and friends (soccer games count), reading, walking, taking a nap. I can do this without guilt, because I tell myself I'm doing it for religious reasons.

But while I love Shabbat, I'll admit that observing it takes discipline. I have no problem taking it easy for a couple of hours, but a whole day? That takes effort.

Often, by the afternoon, I feel out of sorts. My inclination is to "do" something, be productive in some way. I have to remind myself that it's OK just to "be," even if that means I just look out the window and breathe.

On this one day, at least, I don't have to be busier than anybody else.

Nov. 1, 2014

Women can model religious chutzpah

Some people say they aren't religious because religion "does more harm than good."

I'm always stunned by this analysis. The reason: It's a sweeping denunciation of women.

Statistically, women are more religious than men. They have greater faith in God, pray and attend services more often, claim that religion is very important in their lives.

And they also do most of the work.

Women teach the children, work with the teens, organize the adult education, feed the homeless, take care of the elderly, comfort the bereaved, cook the food, plan the holiday celebrations, coordinate the fundraising events . . . you name it, women are there. As I heard one Christian pastor say recently, "The ratio of women and men at the foot of the cross was four to one — and it's been that way ever since."

So while I'm sure the religion naysayers are referring to the wars, intolerance and oppression sometimes associated with religion in the news, to me the real work of religion goes on in day-to-day interactions that don't get much fanfare.

Yet I have to admit, the naysayers are also right.

Globally, religion doesn't correlate with women's equality. According to statistics from the World Values Survey, the more religious a country is, the less equality women have. This remains true even when researchers controlled for demographic characteristics and a country's GNP.

It reminds me of the story of the Little Red Hen, but with a different ending. Women plant the seeds, harvest the crop and make the bread. They just don't get to eat it themselves.

A recent example of continuing oppression is in Israel, a supposedly modern, democratic country. For years, women were not allowed to pray at the Western Wall, one of the holiest sites for religious Jews. When they tried, they got pelted with eggs, chairs and insults. As recently as 2009, a woman was arrested for wearing a tallit, a Jewish prayer shawl, traditionally worn only by men.

The reason women were banned from the Wall is the power of the Ultra-Orthodox in Israel. Even after the Supreme Court ruled in 2013 that women could hold services there, religious leaders said women still couldn't read from the Torah. One bold bat mitzvah girl, Sasha Lutt, thumbed her nose at that. In October, she and a group of women snuck a tiny Torah scroll into the Wall area, where she read her Scripture portion using a magnifying glass.

In other "religious" countries, the oppression is even more severe. Women have less access to jobs, education, political power and health care.

But it doesn't have to be this way. Most religions were born out of a desire for more freedom and liberation, for more righteousness and justice. We must claim these core values and put them to work for women.

The first thing we need is more female leadership. Even in this country, where women have a lot of choices, the number of women clergy has stagnated at about 10-12 percent for almost 20 years. Again, there's a disconnect. If women fill up the pews in almost every congregation and do most of the work, there should be a lot more women leaders.

Laywomen, too, need to step up. As Sheryl Sandberg, COO of Facebook, has urged women to do in their professional lives, religious women need to do in their spiritual lives — lean in. We need to go beyond cooking and organizing events, and start making decisions about our congregation's resources and direction. We need to interpret Scripture and champion social actions that empower women, becoming a prophetic voice of justice.

And we can thumb our noses at unjust religious constraints, modeling the chutzpah of Sasha Lutt.

We make the bread; we can eat it, too.

Nov. 29, 2014

A holiday tale of a girl, her dogs

There once was a girl who loved dogs.

Not just her own dogs, but every dog in the neighborhood.

She'd streak out of the house in the late afternoon, her two dogs in tow — Marlow, a black Yorkie mix with large pointy ears, and her beloved Allie, a shaggy, brown, pint-sized terrier.

The minute her feet hit the park, her eyes scanned the horizon for the other dogs — Monte and Frea; Henry, Penny, Yogi and Graci; Diego and Sylva; Maya, Piraya and Bettick.

She knew all their names, their quirks and skills, their antics and needs. She'd throw them balls, chase them around in circles, retrieve them from a nearby creek. She ran as fast as they did, her 12-year-old coltish legs streaking across the wide-open field.

This was her world.

It was the one place her parents let her go alone. They were skeptical at first. They worried about her safety and who else might show up at the park. But the dog owners, enthralled with this delightful girl who befriended animals, acted as a protective shield against any accidents or unwanted attention.

It was only when the sky grew gray and the tree branches turned black against the dying light that her parents would listen for her return — the clunk of her shoes thrown in the closet, the yip of Allie at her heels. A few times, when the first twinkling star could be seen in the sky and she wasn't home, they'd yell her name from the front porch until they saw her whirling back down the street toward them.

These days her parents worried less about her going to the park and more about when she would stop. How much longer could these magical afternoons last?

"I'm just too tired to go," she might say one day.

Instead of grabbing the dog leashes and rushing out the door, she might retreat to her room to brood or listen to her iPod.

The parents knew how quickly things could change. They had seen it happen before. They had two older children.

But it hadn't happened yet with their youngest. And they were grateful.

One day recently, the girl came home flushed and breathless.

"Look what they gave me!" she said as she thrust an envelope into her mother's hand.

It was a holiday card with a generous gift certificate for iTunes. It was signed by nine people along with the inscription, "Happy holidays from your 'dog park' family!"

"Can you believe it?" she asked, her eyes shining.

The mother's heart squeezed with bittersweet joy. The girl just kept smiling.

It was the best gift ever for the girl who runs with dogs.

Dec. 21, 2014

Marriage is changing for everyone

It's the best of times and the worst of times for marriage.

So says Stephanie Coontz, author of "Marriage, a History." For many couples, marriage is more joyful, loving and satisfying than at any other time in history. It is also more optional — and therefore more fragile — than ever before.

And now gays and lesbians in Florida are going to get a crack at it. On Jan. 6, gay marriage became legal throughout the state.

The news electrified not only the gay and lesbian community in Leon County, but the community as a whole. My wife, Terry, was at the Clerk of Courts Office snapping pictures and rejoicing with those standing in line as the first couples received their marriage licenses.

We received hundreds of likes and comments on our Facebook page congratulating us that our 30-plus-year relationship was now finally legally recognized. At the end of the week, we stood with about 50 others, tears in our eyes, as two women who had been together 23 years got married at Dorothy B. Oven Park.

But the opening of the marriage gates was also sobering. As I said to a friend recently, it's ironic that while gays and lesbians are pounding on the doors to get in, many heterosexuals, particularly young people, are opting out.

For millennia, marriage was about power, property, extending the labor force and creating political alliances, Coontz says. About 250 years ago, the idea of marrying for love — not parental interests — emerged and then took hold, although rigid gender roles were still enforced until the middle of the 19th century. Starting in the 1970s, marriage underwent another radical change — gender roles began crumbling.

Today the main reason people remain married is for mutual self-actualization. If one or both people feel stymied in any major way, the chances of the marriage remaining intact are slim.

In her *New York Times* article, "The Disestablishment of Marriage," Coontz writes: "Marriage is no longer the only place where people make major life transitions and decisions, enter into commitments or incur obligations. The rising age of marriage, combined with the increase in divorce and cohabitation since the 1960s, means that Americans spend a longer period of their adult lives outside marriage than ever before."

How will gays and lesbians fare in these tumultuous marriage waters?

So far, we've reflected that good times/bad times phenomenon. One study followed gays and lesbians — and their heterosexual siblings — over a 10-year period after gay marriage was legalized in Vermont. In it, gays reported greater happiness in their marriages, but they also divorced more often than their heterosexual counterparts.

Terry recently reminded me of a description of marriage she once heard — it's like a fine wine glass. The cup part could provide much enjoyment and fulfillment, but it rested on a fragile stem. Better not break it.

But I wouldn't have it any other way. Despite the stem's vulnerability, the benefits of keeping it intact can be worth it.

Modern marriages require honesty, self-awareness, negotiating skills and affection. The most important thing I've learned is that I have to be Terry's biggest cheerleader — and she has to be mine. Without that unconditional support, it's easy for the marriage to unravel.

I didn't come into my marriage knowing this. I've learned it through our long journey together, including a recent difficult period where we had to renegotiate some basic rules about our daily living.

This past summer, we went on a two-week camping trip together — alone. It was the first time we'd been together that long in 25 years. I was apprehensive. So was she. Would we get along?

Well, dear reader, we did. I found that she was still my best friend, my finest companion. We talked, we laughed uproariously, we sat by the fire at night in comfortable silence.

The stem still held.

Jan. 20, 2015

What children want most is to make their own way

We've made the decision: The treehouse is coming down.

It's been in our naturally wooded backyard for 20 years. And it's a beauty — screened-in main area, slanted roof with real shingles, charming wraparound porch overlooking a stunning sabal palm tree. It took two builders days to put it together.

Too bad our three kids rarely used it.

I learned why when my oldest child was in the third grade. At the time he went to Full Flower, a small, alternative school off Mahan Drive. The teachers gave the kids lots of free time and allowed them to build things outdoors to their hearts' content.

One morning when I dropped David off, he wanted to show me something. He took me over to a large oak tree where he and some other kids had been building a treehouse for over a week. Steps were made out of picket fence boards. The main body was nailed together with various wood and metal materials. A rope slung from two branches sufficed as a handrail.

That's when it hit me: He didn't want a ready-made, beautifully constructed playhouse. He wanted to build one himself.

My two other children, especially my daughter, were the same way. Jenna would drag home all kinds of junk from neighborhood garbage piles — old rugs, dirty buckets, broken screens, worn-thin tires, an off-kilter plastic slide — and construct multiple rooms beneath the trees on the side of our house. Nothing gave her greater pleasure than giving people a tour.

It's a parental lesson that works on many levels — no matter how much we want to give our children the perfect life, the perfect education, the perfect childhood experiences, what they want most is to make their own decisions.

I was reminded of this again recently when I read "Family and Faith: How Religion Is Passed Down Across Generations," by Vern L. Bengston. I was fascinated by the book because one of the most important things I want to pass on to my children is my Jewish faith. Right now my oldest child — he who wanted to build his own treehouse — considers himself a Jew but is not interested in organized religion. I couldn't get my middle child, now 19, to even attend last year's Passover Seder. Will either of them carry on their religious tradition?

According to Bengston, 6 out of 10 children eventually do. This holds true for atheist or agnostic parents — they tend to breed atheist and agnostic children.

It's a statistic that surprised Bengston after studying intergenerational families for more than 40 years. He had assumed most children would have split from their parents' faith.

True, some dropped out for a while. But many came back.

Bengston also found a commonality among the children who carried on the family faith. The piety of the parents or the amount of religious exposure the children got were not that crucial. What did seem to matter was the warmth and acceptance between the parent and child. The greater these were, the more likely the child would remain in the tradition.

I count myself as one of those religious returnees. I was raised in a devout Catholic family, but denounced all religion by the time I graduated from high school. But I came back to religion in my 20s, eventually finding a home in Judaism.

While it's not the same faith as my parents, it matches theirs in terms of intensity. They weren't able to pass on a ready-made religion; I had to find — and build — my own. But I credit them with modeling for me the importance of having a religious life.

I reflect on all of this as we get ready to tear down the treehouse. When Jenna, now almost 13, heard of our decision weeks ago, she was aghast, couldn't believe that we would actually do it. She suddenly took a great interest in the treehouse.

"Can I paint it?" she asked. Sure, why not, we said. It was coming down anyway.

She looked through our old paint cans, picking out colors: light green and lavender. She spent hours over several days slathering the paint on the deck and the support boards, the green paint dribbling down over the lavender. It looks, well, awful, but she had a blast.

Since then she hasn't gone near the treehouse.

The fun was all in the doing.

March 18, 2015

Tragic events can lead to understanding and compassion

I'm a religious person, but I don't believe everything happens for a reason.

True, I may not see the whole picture. And I appreciate that life is often mysterious. But children starving to death? People shot down in their own church?

If there's a reason for that, God has some 'splainin' to do.

Still, I do believe that everything in life can have meaning. Even horrific events have the potential to open our hearts.

There's no need to rush this, just like there's no rush to forgive someone who has done something vicious.

I was moved when I heard the members of the Emanuel AME Church in Charleston say, just days after the massacre, that they forgave the shooter. Wow, I thought, they're way more spiritually evolved than I am. In my experience, forgiveness often comes slowly, over time.

But eventually, in order to integrate a horrible experience into our lives and not let it rip us apart, we need to forgive, and we need to find meaning.

I remember when, almost 30 years ago, my friend, Libby, died by suicide. My first reaction was anger — at God. "I couldn't save her," I cried out, "but You! You could have helped her. Why didn't You?"

For months afterward, despair would wash over me. I was working at a newspaper in Panama City at the time, covering the outlying counties. While I was driving the back roads of Calhoun, Holmes and Jackson counties, tears would suddenly overflow. I couldn't stop crying.

And I was haunted by her final day. That was the store where she bought the gun. That was the parking lot where she shot herself. That was the yellow jasmine that was blooming the day that she died.

But two things came out of Libby's death.

The first was seeing people's facades drop away. Just like the people from Emanuel AME, all of Libby's friends wanted to gather, to talk, to hold one another. I remember one woman in particular. We had never been close, never "clicked." But one night we talked for an hour straight, no awkwardness, no ego. Just two women, open and grieving.

That experience taught me that we have the capacity to connect to one another on a much deeper level than we usually allow ourselves to. That connection gets lost in the day-to-day busyness of our lives, in the walls we build to protect our tender hearts.

The second thing is that I've now experienced a sudden, violent death: the craving for information; the need to repeat the story, over and over; the reliving in my imagination of those last horrible moments.

My compassion for others in similar situations has grown. I've forgiven God. I've forgiven myself.

In the end, Libby's death helped me open up rather than shut down. That's not the reason she died, but it's part of the meaning left behind.

July 23, 2015

Women need a cave of their own

Every woman needs a cave of her own.

Not, however, for the same reasons men do.

"Man caves" — spaces in the house where men can retreat to drink beer, play pool, watch TV, hang antlers on the wall and leave crumpled hamburger wrappers on the end table if they darn well want to — have gained in popularity over the last decade. The idea is that women dominate the rest of the house with womanly decorations and needs. Man caves are the "last bastion of masculinity."

But women don't need caves to get in touch with their femininity. We need them for psychological freedom.

Women tend to be the emotional magnet in a household, with other family members buzzing around, always needing something, interrupting women's time.

I thought this would be particularly true of women my age and older, that younger women would be better at claiming time and space for themselves.

But it seems to be getting worse.

Women today, especially mothers, feel *selfish* when they do anything just for themselves, reports Brigid Schulte in her book, "Overwhelmed: Work, Love, and Play When No One Has the Time." During the last quarter of the 20th century, mothers' time to themselves or with other adults actually dropped by seven hours a week.

Some scholars say that women who take time for themselves, deliberately leaving the family behind, are "courageous," maybe even "subversive."

Even being married to another woman, I've had to lobby for my alone time. Two years ago, I staked out my biggest claim. My middle child had been out of the house for over a year. I circled his room like a hungry panther, wondering how long I had to leave it empty in case he might return.

Then one day, I said the heck with it and took the plunge. In two weeks, I had cleaned out all of his old stuff, shampooed the carpet, washed the windows, bought a new bedspread and painted the walls lavender.

Then . . . I Closed. The. Door.

Ahhh! Something hard and tight began to unwind inside my chest. I felt I could breathe.

My family dubbed it my "girl cave." No one came in unless he or she was invited.

Since that time, I've watched the growing trend of "she-sheds," sweet, tiny female spaces made out of storage sheds in people's backyards. Pinterest has pictures of dozens of them, in all colors, shapes and sizes. I suspect it's a fad that will take hold.

Six months ago, my son moved back home and took over my cave. My chest constricted, but my mother instincts told me he needed the room.

Then a few weeks ago, just as abruptly, he moved out again. As soon as all his boxes were gone, I raced to re-establish my cave.

I don't know how long it will last. My son may yo-yo back and forth for a while, like many of his generation.

But my soul now knows what it wants. If he does come back, it's time to build a she-shed.

Aug. 1, 2015

Election stirs up the soul of protest

I protested in front of the governor's mansion when Florida electrocuted John Spenkelink after reinstituting the death penalty in the 1970s. I marched for the ERA in Washington, D.C. I trespassed onto a nuclear facility in South Carolina as an outcry against nuclear energy.

But as I got older, my protesting days waned. I held fast to my values, but found I was less inclined to hit the streets about them. I told a friend recently, I don't want to fight, I want to *create*.

But today I am dusting off my protesting boots.

Donald Trump is president and my soul is screaming. I don't need to have the "open mind" that Hillary Clinton suggested we give him. I gave the American public an open mind during this whole election. Even as I saw Trump's rise to power, I felt, in the end, voters would not elect him. They wouldn't be able to sleep at night knowing they had endorsed him.

But they did. I know what Trump is. And now I know what many Americans are — people willing to look the other way, despite virulent bigotry; people willing to be bystanders, as long as some piece of their agenda is met.

I have always hated when people pulled the Nazi card. I felt it was too glib, too overused, levied at anyone we didn't agree with.

But in light of this election, it's hard not to make comparisons. Trump's rise to power is rapid. He's doing it legally, just like Hitler did. He doesn't hide his bigotry. Neither did Hitler.

But people still loved Hitler. Still granted him more and more power. America is not Germany in the 1920s and 1930s. We presumably have more checks and balances.

But for me, as a Jew, as a lesbian, as a woman, as a mom of a biracial child, this doesn't bring me much comfort. People who voted for Trump are not my enemy. Some of them I deeply love, others I respect. I believe we have more common ground than not, that God loves all of us, that at some level we are all part of one another.

But I do not trust you. If they come for me, I now believe that you will turn your back.

Which is why I'm ready once again to march, protest or perform civil disobedience when Trump tries to take away our rights, destroy the environment, lead us into another war.

We do not set a good example to our children by appearing to be gracious during this transition of power. We join the mighty tide of justice when we name what we see — and loudly proclaim, "Hell, no!"

Nov. 15, 2016

Accept the challenge of Hanukkah lights

Why are we here?

To let in more light.

That is the message and challenge of Hanukkah.

Many people trivialize Hanukkah, turning it into a kid's holiday filled with presents, *dreidl* playing and chowing on hot, crispy *latkes* (potato pancakes).

But Hanukkah, celebrated with thoughtfulness, is for the mature adult.

Let's start with the story itself. Unlike Passover, when God is in charge of all the action — hardening Pharaoh's heart, causing the plagues, parting the Red Sea — and the Hebrews are passive followers, the Jews in the Hanukkah story take matters into their own hands.

The Temple in Jerusalem has been taken over by the Greeks. It's been swept clean of sacred Jewish objects and instead is being used as a gymnasium. Jews are forbidden to keep the Sabbath, offer sacrifices or circumcise their sons.

When the king's officer tells Mattathias he'll be honored with silver and gold if he sacrifices to pagan gods, Mattathias balks.

"Heaven forbid we should ever abandon the law and its statutes!" he cries.

Mattathais' sons lead a guerrilla war for more than two decades before they finally defeat the Greeks and take back control of the Temple.

That's when God finally enters the picture. The oil found in the Temple is enough to last in the menorah for one day, but instead lasts for eight.

The message: Only after we take action will God perform miracles. No action, no light.

That is particularly challenging for me this Hanukkah season as I find my heart hardening toward those on the other side of the political divide.

I don't think God wants me to solidify my worldview into us vs. them. But neither do I believe God wants me to sit by idly as the world and our social fabric is profaned.

It's a problem not easily or glibly solved. A reason Hanukkah is for grownups, not children.

Each night as we light the Hanukkah candles, we can probe these questions. How can I bring in more light? What is my part? Will my actions keep the flame alive or blow it out?

The candles themselves can provide inspiration. I always find the first night a little sad. Just one lonely candle on the menorah trying to light up the entire room. But by the fourth or fifth night, the light is more pronounced, and by the eighth night the room is glowing.

At Temple Israel we have a tradition that is even more stirring. Every family brings a menorah to Friday night services and places it on a table near the *bimah*, that platform where the Torah is chanted. Then the lights are dimmed, and a member of each family lights the candles.

Now it's not just one candle or one menorah. It's menorah after menorah, flame after flame, light running up and down the long table until the whole temple is ablaze.

Together we can let in the most light. Only then will the miracles come.

Dec. 22, 2016

Afterword

My son, Noah, wrote this essay for an English class during his sophomore year at SAIL High School. The teacher asked the students to write about a pivotal time in their lives. What he wrote speaks volumes about family, tragedy and hope. I thought it was the perfect note to end this book.

*****

Some people want a car, a bike, a big sack of money. A person with cancer wants only one thing — to survive.

When I was 10, I was running the streets with my buddies, biking up to the Dollar Store to buy candy and cheap slingshots to use against the neighborhood bullies. We would come home to our parents and complain about not being able to stay out longer, calling them buttheads and just being overall ungrateful spoiled brats. But that's how kids should be, to a certain extent. Or rather, they shouldn't have to deal with the horrible tragedies that this world has to offer. Not yet. But we do.

The year that I turned 10, my mom got breast cancer. It came as an explosion to both my moms and my whole family, though I didn't understand it completely. I understood that she was sick, but I didn't think that she might die. I thought my family was invincible.

She started going to hundreds of doctor's appointments, some here, some at Moffitt Cancer Center in Tampa. She wasn't at the house a lot, and when she was, she was usually up in her room lying down, doing meditation or who knows what. I didn't go up and bother her. My Ima, who is my other mom, would constantly say to my siblings and me, "Don't go up and bother her! She's resting." I would often hear "Terry!" coming from the upstairs, which meant that my little sister, about 4 years old at the time, had gone up there to find out what she was doing.

Our family is part of a Jewish community here in Tallahassee. This community is very supportive, especially for the sick. One good thing that did come out of this awful situation was the excellent meals that the Jewish support group provided for us. The meals were mouthwatering, smelling like the air of a restaurant in Italy, making your nostrils flare with the aromas. There were all sorts of cheesy and meaty lasagnas, and even vegetarian tofu dishes. We were fed well.

Shortly after my mom found out she had breast cancer, she had surgery. I could tell that, for her, this was a very emotional and devastating loss. I felt bad for her and also felt bad that I couldn't do anything except help around the house and try not to be a pain. One big thing I couldn't do was be there for her if she needed to talk about it, because she wouldn't tell me much. So I was kept in the dark and couldn't see how serious the situation was. Meanwhile, I was a big pain, aggravation and worry for them. I had some anger issues I was working out at the time, but they weren't really getting worked out. It was fights every night, screaming battles, slammed doors and crying. I became suicidal at one point there in the sixth grade. Thankfully, this passed.

During the summer between sixth and seventh grade, I started a mowing business. My brother, David, who had done mowing before, taught me how to go back and forth, keeping the line of uncut grass inside the wheels of the mower. Cutting grass took my mind off things and became an oasis for me, something I could feel good about.

My mom finally came out alive after a couple of years of chemo and radiation. We were so relieved to be getting things back to normal. Her hair started to grow back, and she didn't have to wear hats and scarves any more.

But that wasn't the end of cancer in my family. A year or so later, my Ima got non-Hodgkin's lymphoma. My parents called me into my Ima's office and told me to shut the door. When they told me, all I was thinking was, "What? Why again?" They said it was stage 4 cancer.

"Now, what the hell does that mean?" I asked.

"Usually stage 4 cancers are very serious, fatal," my mom said.

"But this particular cancer isn't fatal, but it's still very serious," my Ima added.

I was flipping out at this point, though not showing it in my actions. I stared off into space. "Why again?"

But it was happening again. And worse this time, because she had to do all sorts of crap to take care of herself. At the same time, she was working hard to stay afloat in the sinking real estate market. She also worried about me and my studies and everything on top of the hell I was putting her through in my day-to-day actions. All this was piled up on top of her chemo and immense bullshit that she was having to do. I was constantly fighting with her, and then blaming myself afterward about how I should be a better son. I felt awful having to sit in the furnace of my own burning mind.

A little while before my Ima got diagnosed, a woman in our Jewish community who had had cancer died. That was a devastating blow to the community and especially to my buddy, about the same age as me, who was the son of the victim. I had no idea what to say to him, so I fumbled with "Hey, how's it going?" followed immediately by "That was a stupid fucking question!" He laughed a little, probably to make me feel better about being an idiot.

I don't really remember the Jewish community giving us food this time around. But it was time for me to step up and start doing more around the house and build a better relationship with my sister. I was working very hard to work out my situation with my sister so that we didn't fight all the time and could have some fun together.

My Ima finally made it, pulling through after her chemo. Afterward, she still had to go for checkups to make sure she didn't have a reoccurrence.

But we still weren't done with the cancer scares. For about a year, I had an inflamed lymph node in my throat that wasn't going away. I got a biopsy done on it. It's not a big procedure, just getting stuck with a needle to get some tissue to test. But the biopsy came back inconclusive, which means we didn't know for sure whether it was cancerous. What?! More?! I needed surgery to take the lymph node out and then have it tested again. When my brother heard, he said, "If he gets cancer, we're moving out of this house!"

So I had the surgery. It wasn't bad or anything, though my chin was bruised for a while and I had a new scar to add to the collection. The tests results took a couple of weeks, two very long weeks. But the tests came back negative. When the doctor told me, a stack of bricks was lifted off my chest and I could breathe again. I hadn't even realized the weight I had been carrying around. I was happy.

And that's the good thing after all this cancer and scares of cancer — we are still a happy family. And we have so much love.